Employee Selection

Christopher Lewis

Stanley Thornes (Publishers) Ltd

First edition published in 1985 by Century Hutchinson Ltd

ISBN 0 09 158271 7

Second edition published in 1992 by:
Stanley Thornes (Publishers) Ltd
Ellenborough House
Wellington Street
CHELTENHAM GL50 1YD
England

Reprinted 1993

British Library Cataloguing in Publication Data
Lewis, Christopher
    Employee selection – 2nd ed. – (Personnel
    management)
    I. Title   II. Series
    658.3

    ISBN 0 7487 1371–9

Typeset by Cambridge Composing (UK) Ltd
Printed and bound in Great Britain at The Bath Press, Avon

Contents

Acknowledgements

I would like to thank the series editor, David Guest, for his encouragement and comment during the preparation of this book. Also my colleagues, Rowan Bayne, Nick Edgerton, David Hogan, Bob Parkinson and Ruth Sage, with whom I have been able to exchange ideas. My thanks go to Evelyn Tovey for displaying such skill and tolerance in typing the manuscript. Finally, I would like to express my gratitude to the late Frank Sneath, who was responsible for nurturing my interest in employee selection.

Introduction

The *General Household Survey 1982*[1] indicates objectively and without emotion the empirical fact that 'In 1973, 3 per cent of men aged 16 to 64 were unemployed while 90 per cent were working; by 1982, 11 per cent were unemployed and 78 per cent working. This pattern was seen among men of all age groups under state retirement age and changes were particularly marked between 1980 and 1982.'

For women, 1973 saw 2 per cent unemployed with 58 per cent working; by 1982, 6 per cent were unemployed with 58 per cent working. Again, the major change in employment was between 1980 and 1982.

These figures show the direction of the quantitative changes in the labour market, a change which consists of many new qualitative aspects. They also explain the changing issues which now affect those involved in recruitment and selection – namely that unemployment has produced an over-supply of labour which has heightened selection problems at the expense of recruitment problems. In practical terms, attracting applicants is less of an issue, but administration and deciding whom to offer employment to are more difficult with large numbers.

These figures also indicate that the percentage of economically active males (that is, those in the labour force either employed or unemployed) has dropped from 93 to 89 per cent, whilst the economically active females have risen from 60 to 64 per cent. This constitutes a significant change in the proportion of women to men seeking employment, which enhances a need for equitable selection.

It should also be noted that there is a 4 per cent increase in economically inactive males. This appears to be largely caused by the increased numbers in full-time education and training. In 1982, the percentage of males aged between 25 and 29 who had been in further or higher education was 27 per cent. For those aged 40 to 49 it was only 14 per cent. For females the 25 to 29 age group had 35 per cent, the 40 to 49 age group 19 per cent.

This means that those involved in recruitment and selection are now being faced with a labour force that contains more well-qualified people. In general, academic achievement is at less of a premium.

A further phenomenon which must not be overlooked, and which is probably a direct result of increased unemployment, is the reduction in job changing. Between 1973 and 1982, those who had changed their job in a twelve-month period prior to the survey fell from 14 to 6 per cent for men, and from 18 to 9 per cent for women. The implication of this is clear – it has become even more important to make accurate selection decisions. Labour mobility is now less to be depended upon to correct selection errors.

Whilst some of these changes are not big in percentage terms, it must be remembered that they do represent large numbers of people. One per cent of the economically active workforce is almost a quarter of a million individuals – easily enough to affect recruitment and selection activity, especially if geographically concentrated.

A feature of the economic and technological change that Britain (and other countries) finds itself experiencing is the corresponding change in the nature of the labour force. By the mid-1980s, the picture was of declining traditional heavy industry being replaced by high technology and service industries such as those in the areas of retailing and finance.

This caused an imbalance between available skills and job requirements, thus producing scarcity even at a time of high unemployment. Well-qualified technology personnel were an obvious example. It is interesting to note that in 1982 recent graduates in the physical sciences were twice as likely to be unemployed as their engineering science contemporaries were (three times if you compare electrical engineers with chemists).[2] Even in 1988, which was a time of lower unemployment, 36 per cent of organizations reported difficulty in recruiting engineering and technology graduates as against only 20 per cent who expressed the same concern with regard to science graduates.[3] At the end of the decade, as just suggested, there were indications that declining employment was about to change. The effect of this would be to deepen and extend the problem of skill shortages. In addition, the spectre was raised that employers would find themselves no longer in a buyer's market. This would have serious implications for current approaches to both recruitment and selection.[4]

This caution was both wise and understandable given the economic projections at the time. The sudden and dramatic down-turn in the economy in the very early 1990s, however, returned the situation to that of the early 1980s, the big difference now being that skill shortages are harder to find and appear only to exist in small pockets. The financial services sector, which saw such rapid growth in the mid-1980s has experienced the same fate as much heavy industry.

To summarize, the activity of recruitment and selection is now confronted by the following:

Fewer jobs attracting many more applicants.

A need to select equitably – supplemented by the force of law with regard to sex and race.

An over-supply of academically well-qualified candidates.

The existence of shortages of certain highly trained applicants.

In general, this represents a rather different picture than existed in the early 1970s and late 1980s – the shift has been from what was largely a recruitment problem to one of selection. Employers can no longer just select at will whom they wish, and most organizations are no longer expanding to absorb, safely and unnoticed, erroneously selected unsuitable candidates. There is a growing pressure to get selection right.

It is to emphasize this that this book is entitled *Employee Selection*: it is considered that this should now be regarded as the focal issue.

A key aspect of accurate selection is that those who are responsible for it, whether they be personnel staff, line or functional managers, or the owners of small businesses, understand the process that they are handling. This is not an easy task. It involves attempting to predict the almost unpredictable – the human being and how he or she will behave. In practical terms, what does the present and past behaviour of candidates tell us about how they will do the job?

In essence it is the awareness of the nature of the process that equips those involved in selection with the ability to cope with changing demands on their skills. The last fifteen years have indicated, most powerfully, that those working in this area should become 'technologists' rather than 'technicians'.

One problem is that texts on selection often fail to meet the needs of the selector. Some concentrate on the complex issues of human behaviour, presenting a useful description of the body of knowledge. They are of value to the occupational psychologists working in the field, but lack practical applicability for the personnel manager or the personnel student.

Others offer a 'Cookbook' guide, treating both recruitment and selection in a highly mechanistic way. This disguises the true complexities of human assessment. This book attempts to bridge the gap between these two approaches.

Although the issues and methods discussed apply to most recruitment and selection situations, there is a focus on 'office' type jobs rather than heavy manual ones, the justification being that the former are changed by high technology whereas the latter often are removed by it.

There are also frequent references to the recruitment and selection of graduates. These are included because of the particular problems attached to the acquisition of highly qualified employees.

The text is in two sections. Section One – The Nature of Recruitment and Selection: The Dilemmas and Controversies – provides the crucial context for understanding: Section Two – Practices and Principles of Selection – suggests how selection, including the necessary recruitment activities, might be systematically undertaken. It contains many references to Section One, emphasizing to the reader the need to be fully appreciative of the dilemmas and controversies if successful selection of employees is to be achieved.

Chapter 1 poses the basic question: 'What is selection actually trying to achieve?' – an important question as it might be an inappropriate solution to an organizational problem.

'What is recruitment?' and 'What is selection?' and 'How do they relate?' are questions dealt with in Chapter 2. Operational rather than dictionary definitions are offered to avoid confusion and conceptual overlap. The distinct definitions are important when examining the problems caused by scarce or abundant manpower.

As the measurement and nature of human attributes are central to selection, Chapters 3 and 4 are devoted to these topics. Firstly, the major measurement problems is dealt with – whether selection can be undertaken in such a way as to allow the decision to be scientifically derived through the use of statistical methods, or whether, at the end of the day, it comes down to personal judgement. Secondly, what are the psychological attributes, such as ability, interest, and personality, and how are they measured? This part of the book must be read and understood before choosing and using selection methods. An appreciation of psychological concepts need not be restricted to psychologists, but it is crucial that selectors understand the nature of what they are attempting to measure in candidates.

The final selection controversy contained in Section One refers to the right to select versus the ability to select. The appearance in the mid-1970s of legislation to remove unfair discrimination on sexual or racial grounds has focused attention on equitable selection. The employer can no longer reject candidates completely at will. It is reasonable to assume that organizations will increasingly be asked to show that they have the ability to make fair selection decisions. This is the subject of Chapter 5.

Section Two, which is intended to provide practical help to the selector, starts in Chapter 6 by suggesting how human resources can be acquired to carry out both recruitment and selection. It is included in order to emphasize that these are highly skilled activities requiring specialized training. Experience and seniority alone are not enough to make a good selector.

Without a doubt, the most important step in undertaking effective employee selection is to understand the job being selected for. In cases where this cannot be specified, it is important to know what the organization as a whole regards as the important features of a successful candidate. The actual procedures for job analysis are covered in Chapter 7.

The activity of generating a pool of suitable candidates and reducing them to an administratively manageable size is discussed in Chapters 8 and 9. The second of these deals with the process, becoming increasingly necessary, of pre-selection.

Chapter 10 considers selection methods and is intended as a guide to choosing them. It avoids, as far as possible, being prescriptive. Instead it concentrates on the advantages and limitations of different methods. It should be remembered that choice of selection methods has, by tradition, been characterized by myths, shibboleths and ritual – all marks of the undiscerning selector.

Selection methods produce information about candidates. The ways that this information is used in deciding which candidate is the most suitable for the job are fraught with error. Different methods have different sources of mistakes built into them. For this reason Chapter 11 is devoted to the process of selection decision-making.

Finally, Chapter 12 emphasizes the importance of revisiting the original decision to carry out recruitment and selection. The questions that need to be asked are, firstly, 'Has it worked?', and, secondly, 'Has it all been worthwhile?' This chapter suggests ways of providing the answer.

It concludes with a quick guide to what might be causing things to go wrong. It then indicates where in the book more detailed help might be found.

References

1 *General Household Survey 1982*, Office of Population Censuses and Surveys (HMSO 1984).

2 J. Taylor and G. Johnes, 'Graduating for the dole', *The Times Higher Education Supplement* (Times Newspapers 6 July 1984).

3 H. Connor and S. Canham, *Graduate Salary and Vacancy Survey* (Institute of Manpower Studies 1988).

4 P. Herriot, *Recruitment in the 90s* (Institute of Personnel Management 1989).

Section One
The Nature of Recruitment and Selection: The Dilemmas and Controversies

This section is designed to provide the essential context which is necessary in understanding the significance of recruitment and selection methods. It should be read before contemplating a recruitment or selection activity. It considers the organizational, scientific, ethical and legal context and sets out to correct popular misconceptions about selection and recruitment.

1
Solving organizational problems through recruitment and selection

Recruitment and selection began at the point in pre-history when, for the first time, the practice of choosing army-style 'volunteers' coincided with the manifestations of the division of labour. Since then, at a very simple level, it has been the solution of organizational problems which has set a recruitment and selection machine in progress.

The idea that if you bring in new people to replace existing staff, you will cure the many organizational ills has a great deal of emotional, if not logical, weight behind it. Indeed, it has frequently brought about the intervention of legislation to keep this feeling in check. It is necessary, by way of introduction, to examine the wider context in which recruitment and selection exists. As an activity it is not isolated, but it clearly has implications for every aspect of an organization's existence.

The notion of acquiring human resources

Any organization, be it business or otherwise, is merely a blueprint for human activity and requires people in order to function.[1] The acquisition of human resources can clearly be brought about through recruitment and selection – this book is devoted to this activity. However, it must be emphasized at this early stage that it is certainly not the only method of acquisition and this should not be overlooked in identifying the need to undertake a recruitment and selection programme. Recruitment and selection increases or changes human resources by bringing in new people, either to expand the organization, or to replace those already there. These new people will, we hope, bring with them additional knowledge, skills or attitudes, which we hope will be manifested in desirable behaviours, that is, what they actually do will be beneficial in helping the organization to achieve its objectives. These desirable behaviours might, however, be brought about in other ways. If we consider, for example, a business organization with the desirable behaviours being higher quality and quantity of output, then the other methods could be:

- *Allocation* – the capacities and inclination of existing members of the workforce might be better utilized if the work was re-allocated.

- *Training* – behaviour can be changed by enhancing knowledge, improving skills, and modifying attitudes through training.

- *Method and equipment design* – quality and quantity might be improved if the jobs and/or equipment are redesigned. Considering a re-allocation of the human and machine contribution to the completion of the task could be an example.

- *Rewards* – the desired behaviour change might be brought about by offering increased financial rewards and incentives. Altering the non-financial rewards might also be a possibility, that is giving job

---

Example 1.1

A commercial organization operating in Central London is experiencing a high turnover of typists – clearly a human resource problem. Approaches to seeking a solution could be:

1 The range of jobs that typists are required to do for the same grade within the organization might be quite varied. Some jobs, for example, might require an ability to handle difficult layouts, others might require an ability to handle difficult narratives. It might therefore be possible to reduce turnover by considering, firstly, which typists had the ability most suited to the nature of the task and, secondly, which typists would prefer to do which of the tasks – *allocation*.

2 It might be that typists entering the organization for the first time are being asked to carry out tasks which would be very new to them since they had not worked with the organization before, and it might be that they are given very little help with how to cope with these tasks, a burden which they carry with them and which in the end causes them to quit. This could be resolved by improving the *training*.

3 Similarly, the equipment that they are asked to use could possibly be very outdated, or could be highly advanced in terms of the technology involved. This, of course, has implications for training, but nevertheless it could be that the equipment is totally inappropriate to the tasks that the typists are being asked to perform. Whilst the company may pride itself on the microprocessor technology it has installed in the form of word processors, for typists the benefits of retrieval and correction might be far outweighed by the irksome continual use of the visual display unit, and this might be the cause of them resigning from their jobs. Similarly, the actual design of the job might be an important factor. One of the effects of microprocessor technology in offices is to alter the division of labour between, for example, the dictator of the letter and the typist of the letter. The technology can bring about either an increase or a decrease in the responsibility that the typist has. This might be unrecognized and might be yet another reason why they are resigning from their jobs. Clearly,

incumbents higher status, improving their self-esteem, giving them more autonomy, or simply less routine.

- *Organizational climate* – some all-embracing characteristics of the organization might be acting against the desired behaviour, that is, the decision-making process might be too undemocratic, or the reverse, thus representing an inappropriate managerial style. It is worth considering the possibility of changing this.

All of the above, along with recruitment and selection, are therefore ways of putting the dynamic 'people' element into the organization

---

therefore, another approach to the problem is to consider *equipment and method design*.

4 It is possible that the organization is experiencing a high turnover simply because it is not paying these staff enough, and this could particularly be a problem in areas where there are many competing employers, as in any commercial centre. If this is the case, then the organization must decide if it can afford the easy solution. It might also be that typists are leaving because, in this particular organization, the job they have to do is rated as very low status, as extremely dull, with much routine, and offering little freedom because of close supervision. Thus modifying either the financial or non-financial *rewards* is a possible solution to the problem.

5 The reason for the high turnover could exist within the more covert aspects of the organization. The overall management style, the attitudes which members of staff experience and are expected to display, and the behaviours which are either rewarded or punished by the organization might be unacceptable to a large proportion of the population from which the typists are recruited. Therefore, attempting to alter the *organizational climate* might go some way to resolving the problem.

6 This issue of high turnover does suggest that it is because the wrong people have been brought into the organization to do the job. One solution might lie in attracting a larger and possibly different pool of applicants who would like to do the job, and then making sure that from these the most suitable people are chosen. Here, clearly, suitability would include being less likely to quit the job. Improved recruitment and selection methods for typists are therefore yet another possible solution to the problem.

Why this particular work group should have this particular problem could, of course, be a combination of one or more of the above, and for that reason none of the solutions are mutually exclusive. However, the example does serve to illustrate that recruitment and selection is just one of several ways of resolving problems with regard to human resources. This, therefore, raises the question 'In what way should it be used?'

blueprint. In practice, however, it is not usually an overt desire to acquire human resources that fires recruitment and selection activity, but the need to solve a problem concerning people and their work. In other words, organizations rarely acquire people without this being seen as a solution to some present or future problem. An example of how recruitment and selection relates to other methods is given in Example 1.1.

The pros and cons of using recruitment and selection

Many of the arguments in favour of using recruitment and selection to solve organizational problems are based on the difficulties of using the other methods. To undertake a programme of job re-allocation often requires an audit of the abilities of existing staff. Whilst personnel records and appraisal reports go some way in allowing this to happen, it is nevertheless a difficult task to undertake in terms of accuracy, and is often politically a very sensitive area.

Training can only offer mixed advantages. Knowledge can be increased quite successfully and levels of skill can be improved provided that the job is fairly repetitive and contains a lot of manual activity. Once the job becomes non-repetitive and requires the incumbent to make decisions or to be creative, then the effect of training is far more questionable. As far as modifying attitudes is concerned, firstly, it is difficult to actually achieve this and, secondly, even if it is achieved it is difficult for attitudes to be converted into behaviour in an enduring way. This is particularly the case in management training.[2]

The problem with method and equipment design is that this can involve the use of logically acceptable hardware which does not actually exist, and which has the further disadvantage of causing a heavy capital expenditure, which presents a particular difficulty if it is to replace or modify what has only recently been installed. One fears that this may increasingly become a problem, especially as computer-based systems are introduced into large commercial organizations.

The use of financial rewards to solve human resource problems is the most widespread form of response, largely because of the ease of administration. It is, of course, particularly prevalent where business organizations, operating in a highly competitive market, are forced to uphold a technology which makes it difficult to introduce non-financial incentives, the clearest example being, perhaps, the motor industry. The price that is paid for this ease of administration is that often only a short-term solution is being offered. Non-financial rewards, usually in the form of job enrichment programmes, are difficult to design, cumbersome to negotiate, and certainly not always successful.[3]

Finally, the idea of changing an organization's climate is dogged by the difficulty involved in getting a clear understanding of from what and to what it is to be changed; it demands support from the very highest levels in the organization; it is also attempting to change the values, attitudes and beliefs of individuals who might be unwilling to change. It can turn out to be a very expensive failure.[4]

Recruitment and selection does appear to be free from most of the problems discussed above, which immediately makes it a very attractive option for the solution of organizational problems. But there are points that need to be borne in mind. Firstly, most of the disadvantages mentioned occur because of conflicting pressures from elsewhere in the organization, which in themselves highlight a problem and are a function of an organization's imperfection. Secondly, recruitment and selection have disadvantages all of their own. The largest merit of recruitment and selection as a method of acquiring human resources would be almost unchallenged if organizations were free to operate an unbridled hire and fire policy, but because of moral and legal considerations (to be discussed in Chapter 5), this is not the case. Because a business organization is not completely free to hire whoever it wants, or dismiss whoever it wants, when it chooses, recruitment and selection as a problem-solving method can get it wrong.

Whilst other methods are perhaps more difficult to administer and are relatively impotent at solving problems, they are less likely to actually make them worse. For example, it might be decided that to solve a technical problem it is necessary to recruit a technical expert. If this person subsequently turns out to be unsuitable, the organization is not only left with the technical problem, but has the added burden of how best to employ this probably highly paid individual. Another example might be the decision to employ older workers in order to remove a problem of absenteeism and lateness experienced with younger workers, only to find that they are unable to adapt to ever changing new technology. Underlying both of these examples is the fundamental disadvantage of using recruitment and selection, namely its inaccuracy.

Recruitment and selection methods in terms of their ability to predict future performance have, to say the least, a poor track record (see Chapters 3 and 10). The reason for this is that so much of the task is concerned with trying to measure such intangible human attributes as capacities or abilities and inclinations or motivations. The difficulties that assessing or even describing these can present are probably most vividly demonstrated by observing the efforts of well-intentioned school teachers as they compile end of term reports for each of their pupils. The inaccuracy in recruitment and selection is not even something that can be significantly corrected by a heavier financial investment. Also, methods are rarely evaluated, largely because those who are actually responsible for carrying out the recruitment and making the selection decisions are not those who have to live with the selection mistakes or are even aware of them. Even if some sort of evaluation is carried out, it can only be on the successes or failures of those selected; in other words it is impossible to judge how successful those who were not selected would have been. Unlike the angler, the recruiter rarely boasts about the 'one that got away', for this would act to remind him or her of the shortcomings of the practice in which he or she is involved.

On balance, the activity of recruitment and selection does have quite a lot going for it as a way of solving the human resource problems which an organization may face, as long as objectives are identified and the best ways of achieving them are well considered – the practice to which this book is devoted. But, as has been pointed out above, it does carry with it the danger of possibly making the problem worse. It is therefore perhaps worthwhile to dwell on this for a moment.

The cost of poor recruitment and selection

The most convenient way of illustrating this is to consider it in terms of attracting and then hiring the wrong person. Looking at it financially, we can take as an example the large organization which employs a large number of new graduates each year. If it makes the wrong selection decision, it will employ an individual who is not going to meet the organization's expectations of an entrant at this level. Because of legal constraints and the unfavourable economic climate, the organization is unable to remove him and he is unwilling to seek employment elsewhere. They are then saddled with an individual whom they do not really want, for the duration of his working career. To tot up his salary for this period, together with costs for any bad decisions that he might make and also, and perhaps more importantly, the costs of the good decisions which the right person, who was kept out by his appointment, would have made, then it is quite easy to crudely guess, even at 1984 figures, that we could be arriving at somewhere between £250,000 and £500,000 for that wrong selection decision. It would, of course, be impossible to accurately cost poor selection in this way. However, even if the individual in the example was just one of a hundred or more hirings, a dramatic point is made, which is that if recruitment and selection is going to be used in the way that it has been discussed in this chapter, then it is worth making every effort to make the best possible job of it. Even to correct only some of its shortcomings could pay handsome dividends. To sum up, recruitment and selection as a method of solving human resource problems within an organization has the distinct advantage of being relatively free from the contamination of organizational conflicts and, in the short term, is an attractive option, but there can be organizational implications in the longer term.

The effects of organizations of recruitment and selection strategies

Trying to solve human resource problems by any means can create other problems. With recruitment and selection it might be that the decision has been made to alter significantly the age range or the level of qualifications for certain types of jobs, brought about by changes in supply and demand in the labour market. The effect of this, however, is to make newcomers different from the existing job incumbents and is a possible source of organizational conflict. In order to attract a particularly scarce skill, it might be necessary to artificially inflate the salary, putting it out of line with existing salaries in the organization. Or, where there is an abundance of applicants, it might be decided to raise the acceptable qualifications level for entrance into the organization. In both these cases it is quite easy to see that there could be problems arising within the organization in the longer term.

However, it is not only the introduction of definite recruitment and selection policies that can cause organizational effects of this kind, but also the failure to be sensitive to changes in the nature of labour supply. Examples of this are local government and the police force, which are two types of organization which, along with many others, have been attracting graduates into jobs which previously did not attract that level of qualification. Whilst there has not been a deliberate policy to recruit graduates at this level, they are nevertheless there and in some cases might be causing non-graduates in the organization to feel threatened in terms of their own longer-term promotion prospects. Another difficult recruitment and selection strategy which can have a marked organizational effect is to cut back drastically on hiring certain categories of employee. In the early 1970s many large organizations dramatically reduced the number of graduates they were prepared to employ. The serious organizational effects, however, did not show themselves until several years later, when it was found that there was a great shortage of manpower within the organization from which to select more senior managers.

Perhaps the most cynical view of the organizational effect of recruitment and selection strategy is expressed in terms of welcoming some of its imperfections. It is that those involved in this activity are forever trying to accurately predict the behaviour of those whom they actually recruit and select. What would happen, therefore, if they got it right? If they got it perfectly right? Those recruited now would be perfectly suited to the organization which we predict will exist in the future, but it is a present picture of a future organization which we know will change in ways that cannot be forecast, and so, by definition, our perfect hirings will be imperfect. This cynical view is then somewhat expanded, perhaps with tongue in cheek, to suggest that it is partly the mistakes in recruitment and selection that allow organizations to cope with unforeseen change. In other words, the capacities and inclinations they hired in unwittingly suddenly have a utility.

Summary

The practice of recruitment and selection must be considered in its organizational context. It is certainly the only strategy available to resolve some human resource problems for example, when there is a need to bring about a large and rapid increase in manpower. However, it is not the solution to all human resource problems and there is a danger that some organizations may not recognize this. One or more alternative strategies, such as work re-allocation, training, equipment design, rewards, and changing the organization climate, might be more effective. Before undertaking recruitment and selection, an organization must confront the question 'Are we sure that this will not cause more problems than it will solve?'

References

1 E. H. Schein, *Organisational Psychology*, 3rd ed. (Prentice-Hall, 1988).
2 P. B. Warr, M. Bird and N. Rakcham, *Evaluation of Management Training* (Gower Press 1970).
3 M. R. Blood and C. L. Hulin, 'Alienation, Environmental Characteristics and Worker Responses', *Journal of Applied Psychology*, 51 (1967), p. 284–90.
4 C. Brown and F. Blackler, *Whatever Happened to Shell's New Philosophy of Management* (Tavistock 1980).

2
The distinction between recruitment and selection

So far, we have considered recruitment and selection as one activity, that which brings new people into the organization. It now becomes necessary to identify the boundaries which differentiate the two concepts. Universally accepted definitions are not available, so, for the sake of further discussion, working definitions are essential. Many employing organizations interchange or confuse the terms, which can hinder common understanding of the activities. I was once invited to travel 2500 miles to a company operating in the Middle East in order to advise on the problems of technical graduate selection. On arrival, it transpired that, out of 125 vacancies, they had managed in a year to fill only one. Selection was clearly not their major problem.

Definitions

It is not uncommon for the practice of selection to be totally subsumed within the term 'recruitment'. Indeed, the derivation of the word renders this reasonable, as it suggests the activity necessary to bring about growth in size.[1] However, we will be better served by working definitions which will be less all-embracing; thus, the following definition is suggested:

> **Recruitment** The activity that generates a pool of applicants, who have the desire to be employed by the organization, from which those suitable can be selected.

Some authors have indicated a dissatisfaction with the term 'selection' as it over-emphasizes the power of the employer in bringing about the contract of employment. In other words, it disguises the fact that, even if a suitable potential employee is identified, he or she may choose not to accept the offer of employment. What is preferred is 'the employment decision'.[2] The problem with using this term is that gaining or losing a good, identified candidate comes under the same heading as the use of different selection methods. Whilst there may clearly be a relationship, which will be discussed later in the chapter, this gain or loss is more likely to be indicative of recruitment methods. For this reason the following definition is suggested:

Selection The activity in which an organization uses one or more methods to assess individuals with a view to making a decision concerning their suitability to join that organization, to perform tasks which may or may not be specified.

These definitions therefore describe the differences between recruitment and selection in terms of the objectives of certain activities. They are not suggesting a simple chronological model, namely that the first stage is labelled recruitment, the second selection. There are clearly selection activities in the early stages – for example, specifying necessary academic qualifications in job advertisements – and recruitment activities in the later stages – for example, using a selection interview to persuade a good applicant that he ought to join your organization.

The value of these working definitions is twofold. Firstly, they make it easier to identify the range of solutions to recruitment and selection problems, such as highlighting the futility of developing highly sophisticated selection methods that throw up extremely acceptable candidates who in the end reject the offer of employment. Secondly, they emphasize that they are both constituent parts of the process, that is, no matter how abundant or scarce the supply of good applicants, both must be taken notice of. However, the distinction between the two takes on a special importance when dealing with the nature of the labour market.

The problem of scarce manpower

Many would see the problem of scarce manpower to be so rapidly disappearing that they would query why it is being discussed here. The fact that its decline is a marked feature of the world economy during the 1980s, and into the foreseeable future, should not hide the fact that there are now, and are likely to be for a long time, severe shortages of certain types of skill. One shortage which has faced British industry during the late 1970s and early 1980s has been certain types of academically qualified engineers. When these scarcities occur, the process of trying to acquire these people must allow recruitment considerations to dominate but not to monopolize. What is needed is to find ways to maximize the size of the pool – firstly, the total pool available to all employers, and secondly, your pool at the expense of your competitors. Examples of strategies readily spring to mind (and these will be discussed more fully in Chapter 8), for example, increasing or changing the nature of advertising used. Several large multinational companies have used corporate prestige advertising on television, which has partly been aimed at enhancing the recruitment of certain types of employees. Other examples are making publicity materials more attractive, and modifying starting salaries, working conditions, or fringe benefits. Less obvious, however, is the scrutiny of selection methods in order to understand their effect on recruitment. It has been demonstrated that the nature of the selection method used contributes considerably to an applicant's acceptance of a job offer.[3] How effective each of the above strategies might be in enhancing recruitment is not easy to identify. It requires trial and error and learning from experience. How difficult this is is illustrated in Example 2.1.

Example 2.1

In 1982 the national output from British universities of graduate engineers of certain categories, available for employment, was 1200. At the same time there were over 200 organizations seeking to employ graduate engineers, with many having several dozen vacancies. One large company, at least, was faced with the problem of not only beating their competitors in the scramble for these hirings, but, if the ratio of applicants to final job offers was to be consistent with other disciplines, they had to attract applications from every engineering graduate! The optimum recruitment strategy in this case is not that easy to identify.

The example does, however, raise a crucial issue. While recruitment is where the emphasis is needed, is selection to be seen as being not really a problem? The answer should be carefully considered. If the number of applicants is not achieved, then the result is either a lowering of standards by modifying the terms of selection, or not achieving the number of hirings required. In the short term the former is the easiest and therefore the most common course of action. However, in the longer term it might not be wise. What are the implications for the organization over time of employing people of lower academic ability than you would normally have been happy to accept? It is a situation where a careful evaluation of recruitment and selection as a method of acquiring human resources, as discussed in Chapter 1, needs to be undertaken.

One problem underlying scarce manpower is that it may be qualitative rather than quantitative in nature. The result is that scarcity goes unnoticed until it is too late. An example of this was the sizeable banking organization which wished to enter the graduate recruitment market in the mid-1970s. It recognized that graduates in total were in plentiful supply and, as it was not particularly concerned about the subject being studied, it was considered unnecessary to embark upon the expensive practice of touring university campuses in order to interview applicants. Instead it placed a quarter-page advertisement in a national daily paper around the end of the academic year. It produced a large response, in fact nearly twenty applicants for each vacancy. They carefully selected the best of the applicants, but nevertheless were disappointed with what they saw. During the next year, as they experienced the performance of their new hirings, their disappointment turned into almost total disbelief in the value of the graduate entrants. What appears to have happened here is that they believed that they could easily attract a sufficiently large pool of applicants. Thus they had concentrated their efforts on trying to get their selection methods right. However, because of their failure to enter the recruitment process early enough, and their insufficient investment of perhaps both time and money, they inherited a pool of applicants largely formed of those who had consistently been rejected by the other employers. This perhaps serves to illustrate the point that, while the numbers within a category of applicant may be plentiful, those that you would find acceptable for your organization may in fact be in scarce supply. This problem suggests a recruitment solution.

The problem of abundant manpower

It is fair to say that most people will recognize the increasing problems of abundant manpower, although, paradoxically, suggestions for systematically dealing with it are hard to come by;[4] this is certainly something which appears to be raised with greater frequency by those working in the selection field. There are certain types of nationally available jobs in the civil service and local authorities which are attracting tens of thousands of applicants, when the number of vacancies is unlikely to reach four figures. One employer of graduates received 8000 applicants for 200 posts. (See Table 2 on page 122.) Increasingly, therefore, there are more applicants chasing less vacancies. In this situation, recruitment is less of a problem than selection.

This might contradict what some will feel to be the case, that is, if there is an excessive abundance of applicants then the problem is how *not* to attract so many. However, on closer examination, what we see is that it is in fact very dangerous to reduce recruitment by, for instance, reducing advertising or making the job less attractive, as this can act to reduce the chances of attracting the better applicants. What should happen is that a selection strategy should be introduced into the recruitment phase – for example, make it known in advertisements that you require higher qualifications. Selection procedures to reduce the size of the pool in order that subsequent selection can take place is commonly referred to as 'pre-selection' and this is discussed much more fully in Chapter 9.

The effect of having applicants in abundance is not only to allow higher qualifications to be sought, but also to require more relevant experience to have been gained before people join the organization. Indeed, it is possible to raise the required standard of almost any human attribute or ability which is considered to be relevant. However, there is a danger, as discussed in Chapter 1, that the organization might be blinded by its abundance of riches and lose sight of the longer organizational implications of raising such standards.

There is a danger, also, in this situation, that recruitment is jettisoned as unimportant. The pool of applicants will always be there – in fact, more than is needed – but the quality, not just the quantity, remains important. For example, within the more than adequate pool of secretarial applicants is the outstanding secretary, as measured by your selection methods. He, or she, also holds that role in the pool of your employing competitors. Recruitment skills are needed to bring about this hiring by your organization.

Clearly, the juxtaposition of recruitment and selection is a function of the scarcity or abundance of those whom you wish to bring into your organization. In order to operate an effective recruitment and selection policy, it is best to avoid being caught by surprise. This is attempted by matching the assessed manpower needs of the organization against the projected state of the labour supply. This planning has obvious merits, but there are dangers.

The merits and dangers of manpower planning

The claim has been made that human resource planning is as essential to an organization as strategic financial and market planning, and that it can be achieved by systematically going through the steps as follows:[5]

Step 1: Goals and plans of organization
Strategic planning – concerned with public policy, social trends, economic conditions, technology, market conditions, strengths and weaknesses of organization, and projected outputs for planning periods.

Step 2: Current human resource situation
Skills inventory – which assess numbers of people grouped by jobs, department, organizational level, vocation, age, education, in-service training completed, and performance.

Step 3: Human resource forecast
The present workforce – what are the projected retirements, lay-offs, promotions and resignations during the planning period?

Demand for people – what is the demand for employees when the plans and forecasts of the organization have been translated for the planning period?

Comparison of demand and supply – if we compare the above, is there a net surplus or deficit?

Step 4: Implementation programme
What recruitment and selection should take place? Also what about performance appraisal, career planning, transfer, promotion, lay-off, training and development, motivation and compensation?

Step 5: Audit and adjustment
Measure the progress of implementation and compare with the plan, taking corrective action if necessary. Change the human resource plan if the organization's plans are altered. This may include periodically updating the skills inventory, forecast and implementation programme.

Models of this nature offer a self-evident logic which acts as a comfort to those in recruitment and selection, but here lies a danger. A careful, systematic plan can acquire the mantle of an accurate picture of the future. Thus, it becomes more convenient not to deviate from the plan, and subsequent evidence which suggests its inaccuracy is resisted. It was suggested some time ago[6] that planning, especially in the social and economic fields, tends to fail because of an inability to discriminate between enlargement, and, of course, reduction, and change. Many systematic planning models are derived by simply extrapolating from past trends, even recent past trends, but without true consideration of the nature of change. The manpower needs of the automated office would clearly be a concern of planning in a large commercial organization. But it could be that the idea of people setting off each day to work at an office will become, in time, obsolete.

If planning is unlikely to be accurate, and nurtures within itself certain inherent dangers, should it be attempted at all? Clearly the answer is 'Yes'. Some areas of change can be foreseen. One approach that has been suggested[7] is that of the 'scenario method'. This advocates the consideration of trends in society, and how they might affect an ever changing organization. This relatively unstructured approach enables the management of an organization to gauge the effect of these trends and how it might maximize or minimize their impact, or indeed initiate change rather than accept it passively. Planning in this context is possibly nothing more than 'insuring' an organization against the effects of the more damaging areas of possible change.

How worthwhile, therefore, is planning in the area of recruitment and selection? As has just been stated, that which is predictable should not be ignored, and that which is not should be 'insured' against. But even this creates problems. Consider the following possibilities which might have some influence in broad terms on recruitment and selection.

1 Will there be a fall in the number of school leavers?
2 Will there be a growth in the use of microchip technology?
3 Will there be a strong economic boom?

4   Will there be lengthy military conflict involving British forces?

5   Will there be a marked change in the political shade of British Government?

This list is offered in the belief that as you go from 1 to 5 the questions become more difficult to answer in terms of accurate prediction. For example, question 1 can be answered with a very high degree of confidence, as we already have sufficient data to make an accurate prediction. Question 2 is indeed very, very likely, although it is slightly harder to make as accurate a forecast, and so on, down to question 5 which is very, very difficult to forecast with confidence. There is, therefore, some merit in attempting to plan with regard to those aspects that can be forecast with some certainty. The danger that lurks, however, is that all factors, whether predictable or not, tend to interact, and so, if we take the above list, while we know fairly confidently how many school leavers there will be, the actual effect that the fall will have on recruitment and selection might well be determined by some of the political decisions made at the time, and what the nature of those will be is very difficult to predict. Therefore this tends to weaken the value of those features which, in themselves, are quite easy to predict.

Another consideration in how worthwhile planning is, is the distinction between internal and external influences on the future, as both need to be taken note of. External influences are those such as the economy, technology, the law, etc. The internal influences on future recruitment and selection are things such as training, development, succession planning, and job design. The distinction here is that the organization will clearly have more control over the internal influences than the external influences, and some manpower planning can take place in relation to these. However, once again the danger is that any internal influences are a function of the external world.

The benefit for recruitment and selection of manpower planning is clearly to avoid getting caught by surprise as to whether you should be concentrating on recruitment aspects or selection aspects. By being aware of the influences that can cause change, you might prevent the surprise, but it may still be too late to do anything about it. However, more attention to planning might not even present the surprises. An organization which in the mid-1970s carefully looked into the future and realized the important influence that the computer was going to have in the running of the business might have developed a recruitment and training policy which considerably increased the number of people with the ability to write computer programs, the assumption being that the dominance of the mainframe computer would continue. They might now find in the mid-1980s that, because of microprocessor technology, the ability to write computer programs is far less necessary than they had originally believed. They thought they were planning carefully, but they did not quite get it right.

What action should those in recruitment and selection take in the area of planning? The following points are offered for guidance:

- Follow the systematic steps quoted above.

- Recognize that the level of accuracy attainable is likely to be disappointing – sometimes seriously.

- Consider how the inaccuracy might be dealt with. This, in essence, requires that flexibility be built in – an example would be to maintain good links with universities and colleges, even though you predict little future need for graduates.

- Identify how extreme the environmental 'scenarios' need become before your plan starts to be counter-productive – this will provide an 'early warning system' as to when to 'bale out'.

- View the plan itself as a monitor of change rather than a predictor of real, future recruitment and selection needs.

This chapter has been considering the distinction between recruitment and selection. It has been argued that it is useful to see them as two separate but mutually interdependent activities. Where the emphasis should go is dependent on whether there is an abundance or a scarcity of manpower. Whether this can be foreseen is desirable but somewhat questionable. It is perhaps a paradox that organizations seeking to become 'leaner and more efficient' are decreasing the manpower and resources that are devoted to the area of recruitment and selection. The point that is being missed is that, while the number of hirings are likely to diminish, it is becoming more important than ever that the organization gets it right.

A point which has been implicit in this discussion is that recruitment and selection should be seen as the responsibility of the organization which is undertaking human resource acquisition in this way. Outside agencies which offer selection services should be seen as a selection method. In other words, an organization cannot delegate its selection responsibility to another organization. All it can do is to make the definite selection decision that the method it wishes to use is that of an outside body.

Summary

Common usage of the terms 'recruitment' and 'selection' are confused. While, literally, recruitment as an activity embraces the practice of selection, it is more useful to take a working definition: 'recruitment' relating to the generating of a pool of applicants; 'selection' to the choosing from that pool of those to be hired.

The value of these definitions is that they focus the problems of scarce manpower as those of 'recruitment', and of abundant manpower as those of 'selection'.

The need for recruitment or selection strategies can be anticipated through manpower planning. However, the self-evident logic of this should not disguise the inherent difficulties of accurately forecasting future events.

References

1 Oxford English Dictionary.
2 D. Torrington and J. Chapman, *Personnel Management*, 2nd ed. (Prentice-Hall 1983).
3 V. Vroom, 'Organisational Choice: A study of pre-post decision processes', *Organisational Behaviour and Human Performance*, 1 (1966), p. 212–25.
4 C. Lewis, 'Pre-selection: Its Reliability and Validity', paper to the British Psychological Society Annual Occupational Psychology Conference (York 1980).
5 D. S. Beach, *Personnel – The Management of People at Work*, 4th ed. (Macmillan 1980).
6 D. Pym, *Industrial Society* (Penguin 1968).
7 P. Lynch, in B. Ungerson (ed.), *Recruitment Handbook*, 2nd ed. (Gower Press 1975).

3
Selection – art or science?

Clearly an essential ingredient of recruitment and selection is the act of crystal ball gazing, especially within the selection activity. You look into the future to see what sort of employee behaviour is necessary and judge how well applicants perform in terms of this required behaviour. Selection is largely a prediction business.

The prediction business

Everybody attempts to foretell the future. The near, middle and distant future are all fair game, and everybody knows that they are not very good at it. However this rarely appears to act as a deterrent. Although selectors are frequently asking themselves the question 'Is this candidate going to be able to do the job?', they might not readily identify themselves as participating in a predictive activity, complete with some of the inherent weaknesses of fortune-telling. The selector is faced with the same problem as the manpower planner, discussed in Chapter 2, in as much as that certain aspects of a candidate are useful for making reasonably accurate predictions, whereas others offer very little assistance. Similarly, predicting the near future is a little easier than the longer term.

Selection methods concern themselves with trying to both quantify and qualify applicants' attributes, with a view to matching these against the demands of subsequent job performance. Recent job experience may usefully indicate subsequent performance, especially in the short term, but apparent interests and inclinations are notoriously unhelpful in predicting performance, especially in the long term. Those who have to select employees for long-term career employment, for example graduate recruitment officers, often complain that their task would be easier if they could choose people for an immediate actual job which will not change. It is as if they are saying, 'If only I could dispense with this uncomfortable long-term uncertainty, I could make an accurate job of selecting employees'. It is possible to be sympathetic to this sentiment, but it does suggest a certain degree of over-optimism concerning the ability to make short-term selection decisions. The issue is like comparing the relative merits of Nostradamus and Old Moore's Almanack. It is all a risky business.

One of the main obstacles to successful prediction is that a clear understanding of the behaviour and performance that is required of the hiring, whether long- or short-term, is often not available, or at least not understood. The paramount necessity for unambiguous selection criteria is discussed in Chapter 7. For the moment, it is assumed that such criteria exist so that we can concentrate our attention on the fundamental methodological aspects of handling predictors, that is, those features of the candidate that give us clues about future performance and behaviour. Risky though it might be, selection does require prediction, prediction that must strive to embrace two crucial qualities – firstly, reliability, and secondly, validity.

Reliability

In the selection context, this refers to the consistency in the way that candidates for the same job are assessed; for example, if two candidates were being considered for the same post, it would be unwise to assess Candidate A purely on the basis of an interview, without using any selection tests, and Candidate B simply on the evidence of test results, using no interview. Alternatively, it might be seen as equally unwise for the selector to concern himself with only the inclinations of Candidate A to do the job and only the abilities of Candidate B to perform the job. The efficiency of selecting in such a way would be like the success of dressmaking using an elastic tape measure.

Validity

In selection this refers to the need to assess what is necessary for accurate prediction of job performance. There is little point in giving a computer-programming aptitude test if this assesses only the ability to do the test and does not indicate how well successful applicants will be able to do a computing related job. Also, the often quoted ability of individuals to be 'good interviewees' is indicative of a low validity in selection if this ability is not related, as it often is not, to subsequent job performance.

Whether or not prediction does have these qualities does not avoid a further fundamental issue. Should this prediction rest heavily on the use of scientific aids, such as statistical methods, or should it depend largely on experienced subjective judgements – is selection a science or an art?[1]

The role of statistics

There are those who advocate that selection should move away, as far as possible, from the perils of human fallibility and seek manifestly objective methods – methods which rest heavily on statistics.[2] These can be used to provide evidence which increases the scientific credibility of selection decisions.

It is not within the scope of this book to provide an introduction to statistics. The discussion below is intended to illustrate how the selector can benefit from the use of statistical concepts. The detail on how these might be applied is contained in the explanation of validation methods in Chapter 12.

The simplest approach is to take an aspect of job candidates, such as selection test results, school examination passes, or length of time in previous job, etc., which can be assessed in some quantifiable way, and to see how well it relates to subsequent performance in the job. If a valid relationship can be demonstrated using sound statistical methods, then focusing on that aspect and deciding who to select or reject on that basis could be considered as scientifically defensible.

To assess the relationship the aspect would need to be considered as one variable and a measure of job performance as another. The normal way of statistically examining the degree of association between any two variables is to use the coefficient of correlation. The context of selection is no exception.

It is important to note how a relationship between two variables is indicated by a correlation coefficient (represented by the symbol 'r'). It is expressed as a number which can never be greater than +1 or less than −1. The nearer the coefficient is to +1 the more highly positive the relationship. The nearer the coefficient to −1 the more highly negative the relationship. A coefficient close to 0 indicates little relationship between the variables.

The important point is that a correlation coefficient provides an objective indication of how well something like a selection test score actually predicts how successful a candidate will be at doing the job. It would be considered by many people to provide stronger evidence than that offered by a selector who defends the use of a test by his judgement that 'it looks like a suitable test for sorting out the applicants'.

Consider the following, highly simplified, example. A personnel officer wishes to find a reasoning and problem-solving test which she can use when selecting school leavers as office trainees. The test must validly predict good job performance and there has to be statistical evidence to support this.

She has acquired a test and wishes to see if it meets her needs. The test is given to candidates, but the results are not used to decide who to accept or who to reject. Instead they are stored until such time as it is possible to assess how well the successful candidates are performing as office trainees. This assessment is to be in the form of a single rating scale.

The test score of six successful candidates are compared with their job performance scores. This is done by plotting both sets of scores on a graph. Such a graph indicates the degree of relationship between these two measures.

The role of a correlation coefficient here would be to place a numerical value on that relationship to indicate how close or distant it is.

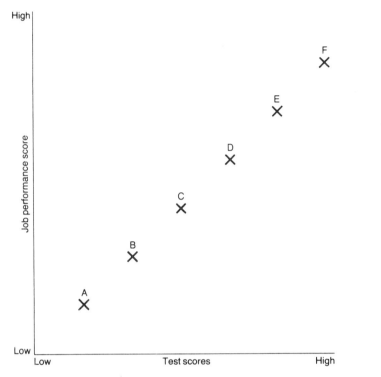

Figure 1   *Perfect positive correlation r = 1.0*

Figures 1 to 4 illustrate examples of four different types of result of this comparison (the candidates are labelled A to F).

In Figure 1 it can be seen that the higher the test score the better will be the subsequent job performance, in a directly proportionate relationship. This represents the almost unheard of situation of a perfectly linear relationship between test score and performance. It is therefore a perfect correlation (r = 1). The test is a perfect predictor.

Figure 2 shows that the performance of the candidates is not neatly, linearly related to the job performance score, but there is, nevertheless, a tendency for the better test score to indicate better job performance, although candidates C and D are perhaps slight exceptions to this rule. The relationship between test and job performance is not perfect, but it is positive. This example represents a degree of association of approximately r = 0.6.

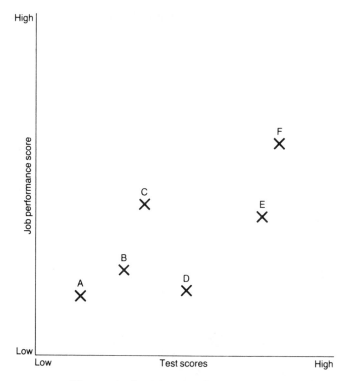

Figure 2   *Positive correlation r = 0.6*

If the picture to emerge was that shown in Figure 3, then this would indicate that test performance has very little relation to job performance. This is shown by candidates B and E who have similar job performance scores but very different test results, and candidates D and F who have different job performance scores but similar test results. Here r = 0.

Finally, Figure 4 indicates a situation where a high test score is associated with a low job performance score, and a low test score with a high job score. In this case there is a negative correlation: r = −0.6.

In practice, the personnel officer would have to use a sample of candidates greater than six in number if statistical evidence on the validity of the test is to be produced (this is discussed later in the chapter). However, if the same pictures emerged, would her needs be met? Clearly the situation shown in Figure 1, the perfect indicator, would be just what she was seeking. It would indicate that there was valid statistical evidence to support a claim that this reasoning and problem-solving test accurately predicted how candidates were going to turn out as office trainees.

If the situation was that in Figure 2, then at least she would know

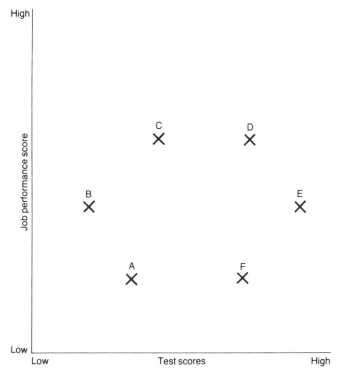

Figure 3 *No correlation r* = 0.0

that the test went some way to being what she was seeking. She could use it in selection, but with caution, being aware of its limitations.

Interestingly, a situation as in Figure 4 would be equally useful. Again, the less than perfect predictive qualities of the test would be known, but this time it would need to be turned on its head, so to speak, with low scorers being seen as better prospects than high scorers.

If the situation in Figure 3 appeared, it would be disappointing for her, as it would indicate the test to be of no value. Ironically, it would also highlight the value of carrying out statistical analysis of test validity. Without it there might have been no way of knowing that the test would have caused her to make random selection decisions.

A real strength in using statistical methods in selection is when reference is made to statistical significance. This results from a procedure which indicates the probability that any relationship between a selection instrument and job performance is 'real' and not just a product of chance. Thus, a statistically orientated selector may make a claim that the selection method being used not only correlates well with job performance scores, but there is evidence that there is a less than 5 per cent

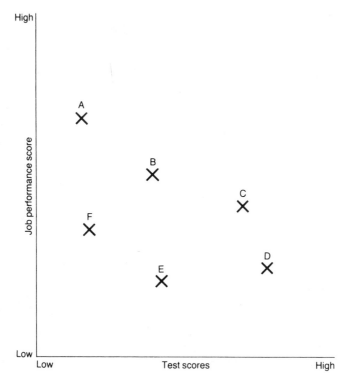

Figure 4   *Negative correlation r = −0.6*

chance that the magnitude of the correlation found was a fluke. Here he
would be talking in terms that had some enhanced 'scientific' credence.

Statistical analysis of the relationship between single selection measures and job performance measures (referred to as a 'bivariate approach')
can be further refined to justify its use. Figure 5 is a graphical represen-
tation of a validation exercise for a selection test (X). The oval shape in
the middle of the graph represents the area in which the individuals
involved in the exercise are spread – the 'scatter' of the cases. What is
represented here is a positive, but less than perfect, relationship between
the predictor variable, that is, the test scores, and the criterial variable,
that is, the job performance score (r = 0.55). High scorers will tend to be
better job performers and low scorers bad performers. But, as indicated
in the case of Figure 2, there are going to be exceptions.

The selector, therefore, armed with this degree of statistical evidence,
needs to take the following steps:

1   He or she can identify the point along the job performance scale
    which represents the threshold of acceptability, that is, the point
    below which job performance is seen as not being good enough. If
    that point was to be identified as being at '1', then all those cases in

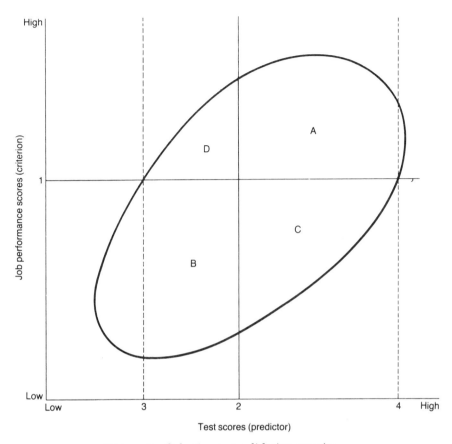

Figure 5 *Selection test validation exercise*

the scatter that come above it represent those people who would actually be good job performers, regardless of their performance in the selection test.

2 Depending on the ratio of applicants to vacancies (this is often referred to as the selection ratio), the selector has to decide what will be the pass/fail cut-off point on the test scores. If we suppose that the decision has been made that it should be at point '2', then those cases occurring to the right-hand side of this point will be selected by the test, regardless of their subsequent job performance.

3 The scatter is then divided into four quadrants, labelled A, B, C and D. The number of cases, or individuals, which occur in quadrant A are not only those which the test would select but those which it would be right to select, as they will perform at an acceptable level (these are referred to as *true positives*). Those in quadrant B are the cases correctly discarded by the test, as they are those individuals

who will not perform to an acceptable standard (*true negatives*). Those in quadrant C are those selected by the test, but incorrectly, as they will not perform well (*false positives*). Finally, those in quadrant D are those incorrectly discarded by the test, as they will perform the job correctly (*false negatives*).

4 The selector can now judge the efficiency of the selection tests, as the number of true positives plus the number of true negatives indicates the degree to which the selection test is doing its job properly. The number of false positives and false negatives indicates where the test is getting it wrong. The existence of false positives and negatives is evidence that the test is less than perfectly valid. (Of course, the higher the statistical validity of a selection test the longer and thinner will be the oval shaped scatter, and subsequently quadrants C and D will be smaller.)

5 A selector can now judge the value of using the selection test as against not using it. This can be done by the following simple formulae. If:

a = the number of true positives
b = the number of true negatives
c = the number of false positives
d = the number of false negatives

Then

$$\frac{a + d}{a + b + c + d} \times \frac{100}{1} = \text{the percentage presently successful not using the test for selection}$$

$$\frac{a}{a + c} \times \frac{100}{1} = \text{the percentage successful using the test}$$

Therefore

$$\left(\frac{a}{a + c} \times \frac{100}{1}\right) - \left(\frac{a + d}{a + b + c + d} \times \frac{100}{1}\right) = \text{percentage utility increase}$$

Thus if, for example, the oval shaped scatter consisted of sixty individuals of whom twenty were true positives, twenty-five true negatives, ten false positives and five false negatives, then substituting these figures in the above formula would give:

$$\left(\frac{20}{20 + 10} \times \frac{100}{1}\right) \left(\frac{20 + 5}{20 + 25 + 10 + 5} \times \frac{100}{1}\right) = \frac{21\frac{2}{3}\% \text{ utility}}{\text{increase}}$$

This would indicate that selection would be over 20 per cent more effective using this test, compared to managing without it.

The idea of demonstrating the utility of a selection test has, in addition, many attractions. Using more complex approaches the utility value can be expressed in direct monetary terms.[3] This is clearly the sort of information that is useful for those who control selection budgets but lack an understanding of selection processes.

6 The selector can also make decisions about whether to alter either the threshold of acceptance point or the cut-off score. In the case of extreme scarcity of certain types of specialists, it might be that false negatives cannot be tolerated, in other words the selection device should not wrongly select out suitable people. The selector will therefore know, because he has evidence of the statistical validity of the test, that he needs to reduce the cut-off point to '3'. This effectively eliminates all false negatives. The price that has to be paid, of course, is that the test is then selecting in a large number of false positives, that is quadrant D disappears and quadrant C becomes enlarged. This was the case in the late 1970s and early 1980s in relation to organizations which were desperately keen to recruit graduate engineers – they simply reduced the class of degree that they were prepared to accept. Alternatively, an organization might consider that it wishes to minimize the number of false positives. It cannot afford, at any cost, to employ people who do not prove to be acceptable. If this is the case then the cut-off score would have to go to point '4'. The effect of this, however, is to greatly increase the number of false negatives. Quadrant C has disappeared, and quadrant D has become greatly enlarged.

Altering the acceptance threshold on the job performance scale is, of course, much more difficult to do, as it is normally related to some change in job design or technology, which may mean that the quality of performance could be lower. It must be pointed out that if that was the case then the selection test might have to be revalidated against the new job design (see page 173).

So far the case for the use of statistical methods has been justified using a simple correlation of job performance with a single selection measure. For simplicity, the idea of a selection test score has been used. This is for two reasons. Firstly, the validity of a given selection test is often queried, and, secondly, it poses problems of quantification. It is easy to compute correlation coefficients using test scores.

In reality, most selection procedures do not use single selection methods, and many that are used are not easy to quantify. The actual selection decision is made, not in relation to the simple bivariate correlation of one selection test with the criterion measurement, but with multiple predictors, with at least one being some form of selection interview. The temptation is, therefore, to assume that the reality of selection decision-making makes it very difficult to apply any notion of statistical rigour. It is one thing to demonstrate the validity of an objective test, but beyond this the scientific nature of selection falls down. Statistical procedures are, however, available which go some way to combating these problems.

The problem of multiple prediction

In order to provide objective evidence through the use of the predictive validity of a number of selection devices, multiple correlation can be used. This is a simple extension of what has been discussed above, namely that each part of the selection procedure is correlated with the measure of job performance. The addition of the correlation coefficients then provides an indicator of the validity of the total selection method. There is, however, a major drawback to this approach – it is only permissible if there is no correlation *between* the various parts of the selection procedure, and it is likely that there will be some degree of association between these parts. However, as will be discussed in Chapter 12, there are ways of overcoming this problem, as far as carrying out the statistical operations is concerned, though they only allow the overlap to be taken into account. The problem that different parts of selection procedures do, in fact, often measure the same thing cannot be changed.

Another way of overcoming the problem of multiple prediction is to consider how important to subsequent job performance are the different aspects of the candidate that are being assessed, for example in the selection of a computer programmer it could be that it was felt necessary to measure *a* general intellectual ability, *b* suitability of temperament to the organization and *c* skill at writing computer programs. Using a simple bivariate approach, as we have seen before, it may be possible to check the predicted validity of the three measures. That would not, however, tell us which of the three abilities was in fact the most important for job success. If the person scored considerably higher than the desired level on measurement *a*, could this be taken to compensate for a performance that was slightly below the required level on measurement *b*? In other words, in terms of successful future performance, how should the three measures be weighted? In statistical terms there needs to be empirical evidence that they are all equal if no different weightings are applied. The absence of weighting factors is not the same as equal weighting, a mistake often made in selection. Hence an important quality of a multiple prediction procedure is that it indicates the various weightings that should be applied to the constituent predictors. A widely used solution is *multiple regression*. This method, unlike multiple correlation, can deal more easily with three or more predictors. At this stage it is probably best to describe it as an extension of correlation, which considers each of the predictors, assesses the relevant weightings and arrives at a single predictor score. At first glance this would seem a mathematically elegant solution to many selectors' dreams. In the case of the computer programmer example, this method would give us a more objective view of the order of the three predictors in terms of their usefulness, and, for any candidate, produce a single score which took these factors into account. However there are problems.

Firstly, multiple regression assumes that each predictor is linearly related to job performance, that is if there is a positive relationship between part of the selection and subsequent criterion performance, then the more that exists the better! At a common-sense level, we know that we cannot always assume this. In the example, general intellectual ability might be the one to be questioned. Very high intellectual ability will not necessarily provide very high job performance.

Secondly, multiple regression operates 'a central trade-off position'. This means it will assume that a very high score on one of the measures compensates for a less than adequate score on one of the others. As mentioned earlier, this may not, necessarily, be the case.

(A worked example of multiple regression in selection is to be found on page 177.)

Problems of the quantification of predictors

As has been suggested, predictors such as tests present the least quantification problems, because tests are normally so designed as to produce a numerical value which measures some attribute of the applicant, but other aspects of selection clearly do not. The data from interviews, application forms and references immediately spring to mind as examples. The problem of initial quantification is, of course, the base line in the use of statistical methods. A crude application of numbers does not provide an answer. The level of statistical sophistication that can be adopted depends on the qualitative level of the basic numerical scale being used. We can consider four levels of scaling.

1 A basic level is where numbers are used as labels or names and this is referred to as a 'nominal scale'. An example of this would be in the classification of an applicant's 'A' levels into subject headings, which might use a system that says call language subjects (1), English (2), Physical Sciencies (3), Applied Sciences (4), Biological Sciences (5), Mathematics (6), Craft subjects (7) and so on. Very few statistical operations can be performed with a scale of this kind, other than count the frequency with which each occurs.

2 A second leve of scaling is what is called an 'ordinal scale', where the numbers do actually refer to some degree of magnitude, that is a higher number indicates something different from a lower number. An example would be the position that an applicant came in his class at school, or in his year at college. It is a scale which provides no more information than the simple rank order and cannot be used in the types of statistical analysis which have so far been discussed in this chapter.

3 A level of scaling which not only measures the degree of magnitude but also uses units which represent equal intervals, namely an 'interval scale', can be used as the basis for the type of correlation

analysis that we have discussed. Examples here are standardized measures, and some test results and examination marks.

4   A final level of scaling is an interval scale where zero on the scale equals the absence of that which is being measured. This can be explained by the phenomenon that a tangible object of zero height does not exist.

The relevance of the scaling issue is that many attempts to deal with the quantification problem of predictors in selection fail to beat this first hurdle. The rating scales used as a measurement of interview perform-ance are often not interval scales, but nevertheless find themselves being built into multiple regression equations. With regard to the interview, one way round it has been suggested,[1] which is that you can ease the scaling problems by reducing the amount of decision-making that the selection interviewer has to undertake. All that is required is that a few well-defined traits are assessed on a numerical scale. These might be such things as intelligence, sociability, personal warmth, etc., with a scale for each. It is felt that, as each scale point is not described, it can be assumed they represent something approaching an interval scale, and can be built in, along with other predictors such as test scores, to form some multiple predictive methodology.

The above discussion may indicate that attempts to take a scientific approach to selection rest very heavily on such statistical concepts as the correlation coefficient, significance, multiple regression, weightings, etc., but really these are just statistical vehicles to demonstrate empiricism. It is saying 'This predictor is valid because objectively there is evidence that it works. Those that do well on this selection measurement do well on the job.' As we shall see in the next chapter, many of the areas that concern those involved in selection relate to human attributes which are vague, difficult to define and difficult to render operational, and therefore we must question the scientific status of the activity; but the empiricial methods which we have discussed can actually bypass this argument by the claim that 'it does not really matter what is actually being measured, because it does predict job success'.

The major threat, however, to a scientific claim for selection lies not particularly in the nature of the predictor, but in the nature of the criteria, the measure of job performance. In the discussion on the use of statistics in selection, the measure for job performance, the criterion score, has been taken for granted. The need for predictors of job perform-ance to be both reliable and valid equally applies to the job performance measure itself. These problems will be discussed in detail in Chapter 12, but at this point it must be said that they are great enough to raise a very large question-mark indeed over the whole area of statistical validation of selection methods. That is not to say that it does not work, but simply to query whether statistical evidence, which is often presented as hard data in justifying the value of a selection method, is really that reliable.

A typing selection test might predict very well job performance, as measured by the quantity and accuracy of letters typed. The test does not in any way indicate what the typist will contribute in terms of harmony, or the opposite, to the work group, a factor that could render the high scoring typist unsuitable for the job. One reason why this factor may not have been included in the job performance measure is that it is an aspect which is very difficult to quantify. Thus the empirical evidence is really saying 'Here is hard scientific evidence that the person who does well on this selection test will do well in one aspect of a job, but we cannot comment on the other aspects.'

Two criticisms traditionally levelled at attempts to demonstrate the statistical validity of selection methods are:

1 That the correlation coefficients produced are never very high – r = 0.4 would be what a selector might reasonably expect to get.[4]

2 That the methods are too situationally specific. If a selection method is shown to have some validity in relation to a given job, it cannot be assumed that this method will be equally valid for a similar job in a different organization. Further, if the content of a job is changed, even to a small degree, the statistical validation exercise would have to be undertaken again. These limitations have acted as a disincentive to bothering with rigorous validation procedures.

Extensive work undertaken in the late 1970s and early 1980s has produced evidence to challenge these criticisms.[5] Both can be attributed to the poor application of statistical methods. The chief offenders are:

a Sampling error – the failure to use an adequate sample of applicants on which to base the statistical analysis. Because there is often no choice, studies are carried out on numbers that are too small, and very frequently on job incumbents rather than job applicants. The number problem increases the chance of the correlation coefficient being a fluke result, the fact that they are incumbents alters the range of people undertaking the selection method from what it ought realistically to be.

b Job performance measurement error – the failure to allow for the unreliability (lack of stablity) of the often crude measures of job performance. This can seriously affect the accuracy of a correlation coefficient as an expression of true validity.

Thus, if these methodological problems can be overcome, then statistically based validity would be greater than usually demonstrated; and would not be situationally specific, but generalizable within 'families' of jobs or even beyond.[6]

One of the problems of a strong emphasis on the use of empiricism, or science, in selection is that there is a danger that it might dehumanize the selection process from the selector's point of view. The idea that you might, for example, ask selection interviewers to narrow down their decision-making enormously, and make only limited judgements is to lessen the weighting given to the value of human judgement.

The role of human judgement

Selection frequently relies on various sources of information. The stastical treatment of these has been suggested and discussed. However, at the end of the day, the selector is normally asked to use his or her judgement. Psychologists have devoted their attention to this problem and it has been couched in terms of statistical versus clinical prediction,[7] the latter term not referring to assessment of health but to the acceptance of the 'professional judgement' of the medical profession as a model for decision-making. Evidence has been offered to suggest that clinical prediction is less valid than statistical prediction.[8] It is this kind of evidence which has given the impetus to the scientific approach to selection – the selectors, especially during a selection interview, must become simply meters, rather than processors and evaluators, of information. However, the accuracy of this has been challenged, especially in relation to the selection for complex jobs such as those of supervisors and managers.[9] The use of statistical predictors, such as psychological tests and the analysis of application form data, have been shown to be of some use in selecting first line supervisors, but of little use in selecting those higher in the organization; whereas clinical judgements, such as assessments made by senior managers and also the use of peer ratings, appear to be 'surprisingly successful' in predicting the subsequent performance of someone coming into a managerial job.

Further, not only has the accuracy of statistical prediction been challenged, so has the logic.[9] Many of the aspects of a candidate that the statistical approach would require to be simply rated on a single scale are themselves very complex. A single attribute like 'sociability' can only be judged by a complex interchange between the selector and the candidate and would normally happen in the interview. To arrive at a single rating, the selector would have to process and evaluate a great deal of information. Therefore it is after all a clinical judgement. Clearly statistical prediction is essential to selection but not at the expense of clinical judgement – largely because it is very difficult in practice to unravel the two approaches. Statistics can give small, precise pieces of information about a candidate, but because of the problem of the remaining, but necessary, pieces of information that cannot be quantified, clinical judgement based on experience is necessary to give the selection process, as a whole, 'real' validity rather than just 'statistical' validity.

A systematic attempt to bring together the art of selection with the science is to be found in the use of *assessment centres*. This is a method of selection or assessment which has its more modern roots in the work carried out at the American Telegraph and Telephone Company.[10] It uses various statistically validated measures, such as psychological tests, structured exercises and job sampling; and the candidate's performance on these is presented to a group of trained assessors who are normally senior managers from the recruiting organization. These assessors have also been observing these candidates during their performance on these measures and during interviews. They are then required to make a clinical assessment of the candidates, based on all of these data. It is a procedure, therefore, which contains statistically validated – and thus scientifically justified – information about the candidate. However, the validity of the whole process depends on the accuracy of the clinical assessment of this information (see Chapter 10).

Is selection therefore an art or a science? On balance, it should be the latter, but only just. Unlike other scientific endeavours, the process rests heavily on experienced professional judgement, but ultimately the resulting decisions need to be examined to see if they have been valid. Unfortunately, striving to produce objective evidence that selection is achieving what it is meant to be achieving involves a commitment in the face of the practical problems involved. Not only is there the concern that those who have been selected will successfully perform the job, but also further issues. What is successful performance? How good would those not selected have been? These issues are discussed more fully in Chapters 7 and 12.

Summary

Selection is concerned with prediction. Which candidate will be best at doing the job? In order to predict, selection practices need to be able to measure certain relevant aspects of those seeking employment. These measures must be both stable (that is, reliable) and accurate (that is, valid). One view is that this can be achieved scientifically by using well-established statistical methods, especially the coefficient of correlation.

Another very different approach is to consider the assessment of human potential to be too complex for statistical analysis. It requires human judgement – this being an art which should be developed.

References

1 C. Lewis, 'Investigating the employment interview: A consideration of counselling skills', *Journal of Occupational Psychology*, **53** (1980), p. 111–16.

2 F. J. Landy and D. A. Trumbo, *Psychology of Work Behavior*, (Illinois: The Dorsey Press 1976).

3 J. M. Prieto, 'Tests of aptitude' in P. Herriot (ed.), *Assessment and Selection in Organizations* (Wiley 1989).

4 E. E. Ghiselli, *The Validity of Occupational Aptitude Tests* (Wiley 1966).

5 F. L. Schmidt and J. E. Hunter, 'Employment Testing. Old theories and new research findings', *American Psychologist*, **36** (1980) no. 10, p. 1128–37.

6 K. Pearlman, F. L. Schmidt and J. E. Hunter, 'Validity generalisation results for tests used to predict training success and job proficiency in clerical occupations', *Journal of Applied Psychology*, **65** (1980), p. 373–406.

7 P. E. Meehl, 'Seer over sign: The first good example', *Journal of Experimental Research in Personality*, **1** (1965), p. 27–32.

8 A. J. Korman, 'The prediction of managerial performance – a review', *Personnel Psychology*, **21** (1968), p. 295–322.

9 R. D. Arvey and J. E. Campion, 'The employment interview: A summary and review of recent literature', *Personnel Psychology*, **35** (1982), p. 281–322.

P. Herriot, 'Towards an attribution theory of the selection interview', *Journal of Occupational Psychology*, **54** (1980), p. 165–73.

Lewis, 'Investigating the employment interview'.

10 D. W. Bray and D. L. Grant, 'The assessment center in the measurement of potential business management', *Psychological Monographs*, **80** (1966), no. 625.

4
The selector as psychologist – the psychologist as selector

One of the problems underlying the art or science issue in selection and recruitment is the concern with psychological attributes. This is inevitable in an exercise which is aiming to predict human behaviour. Thus the success or failure of recruitment and selection procedures can rest heavily on the ability of those operating them to deal with such intangible notions. Words such as 'intelligence', 'personality', 'aptitude', and 'interest', as used to classify desirable attributes for job performance, are commonly found in the selectors' and recruiters' vocabulary, often ill-defined, undeveloped or downright misunderstood. Further, the hypothetical nature of these attributes presents an almost insurmountable measurement problem which frequently goes unrecognized or even uncared about. For example, at the recruitment stage an employer might be seeking to attract 'intelligent school-leavers'. The selection methods will focus on unearthing this attribute and the selection decision will be weighted towards the more 'intelligent' candidates. But what is meant by this label 'intelligence' is never defined or thought through. At one stage it might be equated with educational achievement. But this might be seriously modified, as indicated by such interviewer comment as 'Despite his rather poor school record he came across as a very intelligent young man'. Thus it is now being equated with other things. Maybe something like 'intelligence' is a very complex psychological concept, and requires a psychologist with recognized training to clarify and define it. (This includes, of course, personnel managers who have followed a course in psychology during their professional training and maintained an interest in it.)

However, psychologists researching directly in the field cannot even agree on a definition.[1] Some see it as an ability to reason in the abstract, others as the ability to make optimum decisions in given situations, and others simply as the ability to take intelligence tests. There are probably as many definitions as there are researchers.

This example opens up an interesting debate. On the one hand, as recruitment and selection have to deal with psychological aspects, they should be left to trained psychologists. On the other, can psychologists ultimately make better selection decisions? (Some published psychological tests are only supplied to qualified psychologists or those trained by qualified psychologists – see Chapter 6.)

As has been suggested, the layman might be ill-equipped to understand exactly what is being sought and assessed in candidates. The psychologist should be able to help to overcome this, not by offering precise definitions, but by suggesting ways of coping with the lack of clarity. The topic of intelligence is one such area where lack of consensus in definition has forced psychologists to take a working definition – simply the empirical fact that people differ one from another in their ability to perform tasks. Thus, in a selection context, to identify the tasks in the job and to strive to select the best performer bypasses the need to bother with the woolliness of the term 'intelligence'.

It is probably true to say that the main contribution that psychologists have made to recruitment and selection has been in the area of selection method development, rather than selection decision-making – the problems of psychological measurement in general have produced answers which can benefit selection. The essential properties of such measurement devices can be classified in the following way.

1   *Reliability and validity*   As described in the previous chapter, when applied to selection methods this indicates that, firstly, any selection method must be stable and, secondly, that any selection method must be actually measuring what you want it to measure.

2   *Standardization*   Any selection method must be translatable from the particular to the general. An example would be the organization which is using a computer aptitude test in the selection of computer programmers. Clearly it would be important for that organization to know how the test scores achieved by their applicants compared with computer programmers' scores in general. Thus this particular selection method needs to be standardized against a wider population, otherwise it is being operated in the 'vacuum' of that organization's own selection procedure.

3   *Discrimination*   A selection method is only useful if it discriminates between the applicants. An interview procedure is of little use if it is so tough that all the candidates fare very badly. Similarly, an educational test would be equally useless if all the applicants scored full marks. Selection methods should be designed so that the average applicant achieves the average performance. Thus if a quantifiable selection method is being used, the average applicant should score at the middle of the range of scores. Any deviation from this means that the selection method is either discriminating against the very good applicants or against the very bad applicants.

It is often not easy to recognize if a measuring device has these properties. Selectors may need to seek professional advice from a psychologist before using unproven techniques.

Whilst there are problems with precise definitions of psychological attributes, some useful clarification can be achieved, not only to enhance understanding of what they might be, but also to highlight what they are not. For this reason, some of the most commonly referred to attributes are discussed below.

The nature and measurement of ability

Ability is the nearest to an all-embracing factor which suggests whether a candidate will be able to perform the job. It has traditionally been seen to contain two components, namely attainment and aptitude or potential, but more recently some have interpreted it to mean competence.

1 *Attainment*   This is an assessment of what a candidate can do at the time of selection. What skills will he or she be able to bring to the job on Day One? It is clearly a combination of both education and experience. Many selectors assess these two areas as ends in themselves, but the information collected should firstly be used to assess attainment. When selecting, for example, a word-processor operator, it might be expected that any person selected will bring skills in typing, the ability to operate the machine, and a good command of the English language. There is no expectation by the employer to have to give training in these. Judgement as to whether the required attainment exists rests on the detail of educational achievement and previous job experience, including any training contained within it.

2 *Aptitude*   This is an assessment of a candidate's capacity to be trained or developed. It is not a question of what he or she can do, as soon as they commence the job, but what level and type of performance can be achieved given some development by the organization. Clearly education and experience will provide some clues, but so will evidence of inclination to do the job. In the case of the word-processor operator selection, it would not be expected that the individual hired would immediately be able to handle the documentation and procedures on the machine, which are unique to that organization. What is looked for is an aptitude to acquire this quickly and accurately. Skill acquisition

The juxtaposition of these two components plays an important part when the decision has to be made between selecting for a job, or selecting someone to be trained to do the job – a simple distinction which is surprisingly often ill-considered. An organization wishing to recruit a systems analyst may be fully anticipating to have to train thoroughly the new hiring in the organization's own systems styles and practices, and accepts that some considerable time may have to be devoted to this, although the job is not treated as if it was for a 'trainee systems analyst'.

This can misdirect the selection effort away from aptitude towards attainment, the result being a successful candidate with a sound training and experience in inappropriate systems and a limited ability to be changed to the new ones.

In graduate recruitment the distinction between attainment and aptitude is interesting. The whole justification for seeking highly educated people is normally that they are the potential management of the organization. This implies that selection should focus on the candidate's aptitude to be developed as a manager. For this reason the value of a first-class degree needs to be carefully evaluated against other qualities and experiences, such as organizing and leading, rather than taken as a highly desirable attribute in its own right.

Another distinction is between arts graduates and engineers, in that attainment is probably more relevant to the latter, as the employer will expect to be hiring in some engineering skill.

Whether one is primarily concerned with attainment or aptitude depends on the answer to the question, 'What am I really selecting for?' With an enhanced awareness of an ever-changing, unpredictable environment, abilities such as flexibility and adaptability are identified as desirable. A candidate with a good track record in these is displaying aptitude rather than attainment. This is further discussed in Chapter 7.

3 *Competence* A more recent development has been to challenge the whole concept of ability.[2] A view expressed is that, as a consequence of traditional ideas of ability, individuals tend to be assessed only on a fairly limited range of named aptitudes. This reduces in scope the idea of individuality. Any comparison between two individuals tends to be expressed by their relative performance on a small range of aptitude measures. Candidates, for example, are often compared using only a small number of selection ability tests. The suggestion which is made is that individuals be seen in terms of their repertoire of competences, that is an individual must be seen in terms of what he or she is able to perform. This includes tasks from their work and from their leisure. Every individual will be different, because no two people will have exactly the same list of competences. This notion could be applied to selection by identifying what competences are required to do the job, and matching these against individualized lists, the most suitable candidate being the one with the most embracing repertoire. While this view presents a strong challenge to conventional wisdom in the area of ability and selection, it is relatively untried and untested. This does not mean it should not receive further attention. In the present economic climate, the idea that individuals be assessed in terms of their competences rather than their range of abilities is far more useful in helping them to prepare for long periods without conventional employment. There is

also a growing use of this concept in the analysis of managerial jobs (see Chapter 7).

The measurement of ability

The exploration of education and experience is usually assessed initially from application forms and then through the interview and references. This provides an insight into a candidate's ability. However, ability is also the most common aspect of a candidate that is subject to standardized testing; either in the form of pencil and paper tests which, as the name suggests, reduce ability to something that can be measured by responses to written questions or printed diagrams; or by performance tests, which require the candidates to engage in some predetermined practical exercise.

Attainment testing

Any test which sets out to measure how much skill a candidate can display would come under this heading, provided that the result is not used to assess other skills. A spelling test for typists measures attainment as long as it is only used to measure spelling and not used to predict performance as a typist. Educational examinations are used as attainment tests. 'O' level mathematics gives some indication of skill with figures. A degree in a modern foreign language suggests an ability to understand that language in written form. A university department of chemisty will expect applicants for degree places to have a reasonable 'A' level pass in chemistry. It requires this level of attainment because it does not want to teach its students from scratch.

Aptitude testing

Compared to attainment testing, aptitude testing is far less straightforward. It requires a theoretical underpinning which is often the source of controversy. Much of what is referred to as 'psychological testing' comes under this heading, and it is therefore an area of recruitment and selection which particularly interests the psychologist.

It is this topic which embraces the debate on the nature and measurement of intelligence. As was said previously, the working definition of intelligence is simply the phenomenon that individuals differ in their performance of tasks. Thus, aptitude testing takes the stance that the task of undertaking a test is indicative of differentiable intellectual activity. A debate which has continued during the whole of the twentieth century is whether intellectual activity is an all-embracing affair, that is, is there such a thing as general intelligence? The models produced by British psychologists[3] have tended to support the view, whereas those in the United States[4] have argued that intellectual activity is more task-specific. This debate is important for aptitude testing in selection. The

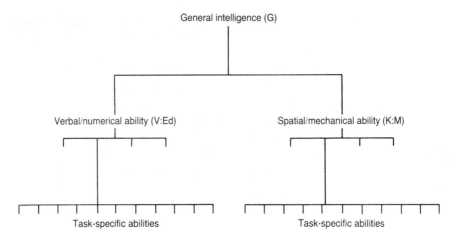

Figure 6   *Aptitude testing model (after Vernon 1951)*

model[5] shown in Figure 6 is one that has strongly influenced the design of aptitude testing in Britain.

This indicates that, in seeking to explain why individuals perform tasks differently, the most powerful influence is a factor that embraces all activities, which is something approaching general intelligence (G). A less powerful influence is either a words/numbers ability (V:Ed) or a spatial/mechanical ability (K:M). A further influence, but again even less powerful, is divisions of the V:Ed and K:M which continue until the bottom of the hierarchy is reached at the unique ability required to perform a specific task in question, this unique ability having very little influence itself on performance. A model[6] which has strongly influenced test design in the United States, suggests that there is little evidence to support the view of general intelligence. If the 'nature of intelligence' is replaced by the 'structure of abilities', then there is a set of discrete independent ability categories labelled 'primary mental abilities'. They are:

Spatial ability
Numerical ability
Memory
Inductive reasoning
Perceptual speed
Verbal meaning
Verbal fluency

The difference between individual performance on tasks is explained by the extent to which the task relates to one or more of these abilities. If the British view is accepted, then it implies that most aptitude testing situations demand the use of a measure of general intelligence, as differences in this all-embracing aptitude are the major explanation why two individuals will perform differently on a given task. More specific aptitude tests contribute less to the explanation.

If the United States model is accepted, then aptitude testing involves identifying which of the primary mental abilities is necessary for the performance of the task, and appropriate tests related to these would be used. In practice, the differences can be illustrated by Example 4.1.

Example 4.1

An organization which sets out to recruit engineering design draughtsmen, if influenced by the British view of ability, would initially test the applicants using a measure of general intelligence, remove those who had not scored at a satisfactory level and then submit the others to spatial and mechanical reasoning tests. Those who had performed at an acceptable level in these tests might then be subjected to specific 'design draughtsmen performance tests', which might well be locally prepared. Suitable recruits would be those who successfully passed each of these hurdles.

On the other hand, if the same job was being selected for, but this time using a more United States-influenced model, it could mean that all the abilities would be tested. If, however, this was inconvenient, selection might tend to focus on spatial ability, numerical ability and maybe inductive reasoning, but it is likely that these three tests would be given equal weight and there would not be the hurdle system that the previous method had suggested.

Trainability testing

Tests designed to measure an individual's ability to be trained, usually in relation to craft occupations, are worth mentioning separately. They are, by definition, aptitude tests, but because they are frequently performance rather than pencil and paper tests, and appear to be measuring practical skill, they are often wrongly classed as attainment tests.[7]

It has recently been suggested that some aptitude tests used to assess trainability can be used in the selection of successful job performers with greater confidence than previously thought.[8] Methodologically poor validation studies have erroneously suggested that to successfully perform a job requires different abilities from those required to be successfully trained to do it. Using a massive sample of 370,000, it was demonstrated that the more valid the test in predicting training success, the more valid it is likely to be as a predictor of later job performance. Employers selecting people who will do well in training are selecting those who will do well later.[9]

The main distinguishing feature between attainment and aptitude tests is therefore not their design but their purpose. The spelling test for typing, referred to earlier, could become an aptitude test if it was found that high scorers became good all-round typists. Also, to pick up another earlier example, the 'A' level chemistry student who applies to university, but this time to read philosophy or sociology, may also be asked for a high grade, but in this instance, the 'A' level examination is being used as a measurement of his ability to follow an educational course. Thus it is a measurement of aptitude.

The nature and measurement of interests

Whilst ability is probably the most important factor in selection, one which commands much attention during a selection procedure, especially on application forms and during selection interviews, is that of interests. Normally, this is couched in terms of hobbies and out-of-work activities. Investigation of hobbies seems to have a strange fascination for many interviewers. This is somewhat mystifying. The occupational relevance of interests that candidates have outside of their work time is difficult to determine. It is particularly striking if you consider the difficulty in answering the question, 'In order to do the job successfully, what interests must the candidate have ... ?' Unfortunately, there is a temptation to actually produce answers which are really quite contrived, like seeking the word-processor operator who spends a lot of leisure time playing with video games.

To accuse the selection interviewer of dwelling so much on this aspect of a candidate simply because it provides more interesting, less routine information, and thus some light relief as compared with the rest of the interview, would be tempting, but unfair. While an investigation of a candidate's interests is perhaps less fruitful in the final decision-making than close examination of ability, there is, nevertheless, some benefit which must not be discounted. However, a problem of definition must be thought through. Are interests to be equated with hobbies? Are hobbies to include pastimes? Is it to be a broader concept to contain everything that the individual does outside his working time? Indeed, should it include aspects of working time which are particularly appealing to that individual? If interests mean just hobbies, then at that level such information is probably at its least useful. Candidates will tend to present their hobbies only if they consider that it will enhance their employment prospects, in other words they will tend to list only those activities which they judge to be socially acceptable. An experienced graduate recruitment interviewer was once heard to remark 'If all those applicants who claimed to have an interest in fell-walking really meant it, then it would be impossible to enter Derbyshire on a weekend because of all these energetic, backpacked undergraduates, saturating the hillsides.' If interests are extended to include all out-of-work pursuits, that is those which might not be seen so readily as socially acceptable, such as just sitting down watching the television, or going drinking with friends, then they are perhaps producing evidence which is useful to the selector. Dimensions such as 'active' versus 'passive' participation, or 'loner' versus 'gregarious' might suggest features of the candidate which are occupationally relevant.

If interests are seen to include work-time activities, then, of course, they become even more occupationally relevant, because it is possible to get some insight into those difficult, intangible areas such as job satisfaction, and inclination. It is this sort of investigation into interests, therefore, which can provide important data for the judgemental aspects of decision-making, discussed in the previous chapter.

The measurement of interest
While application forms normally request information concerning interests, selectors are often sceptical about the value of the interest information contained on them. The traditional arena for the evaluation of interests is the selection interview. However, there are standardized measures of interests. It is incorrect to refer to these as 'interest tests' as that tends to imply that there is a notion of a cut-off point above which you pass and below which you fail. The measurement of interest is very much an exercise to establish an individual interest structure or pattern. The terms 'interest inventories', 'interest questionnaires' or 'interest blanks' are more commonly used. In practice, the standardized measures of occupational interest are found more in the field of vocational guidance and less frequently in selection. Traditional interest inventories require that the person being tested indicates his or her strength of interest in such things as hobbies, recreation, leisure-time activities, job and other activities. A typical mode of format is to present two or more activities and ask the individual which one he likes the most or likes least, or to state how much he likes it.

Probably the interest blanks most commonly found in selection are, firstly, the 'Strong Vocational Interest Blank (SVIB). The premise on which the SVIB is based is that a person choosing a profession or occupation is more likely to be happy and successful if his or her basic interests are similar to the interests of those actually working in the field. Thus it measures whether the subject's pattern of interest agrees with the interest pattern of those in each of a number of professions or occupations. Secondly, there is the 'Kuder Preference Record' (KPR) and the 'Kruder Occupational Interest Survey' (KOIS). The KPR contains triads of activities and, from each, a subject has to choose the most preferred and the least preferred. This form assesses interest associated with ten broad occupational areas, namely mechanical, outdoor, computational, scientific, persuasive, artistic, literary, musical, social services, and clerical. The KOIS allows scoring to be converted into interest patterns of people in various occupations. It is therefore doing the same thing as the SVIB.

There is a general acceptance that interest measurement is a cruder device than the measurement of ability. It is very difficult, if not impossible, to unearth evidence of the predictive ability of interest blanks when used in selection. However some evidence was offered as long ago as the 1950s[10] that the Kuder Preference Record could be used to predict those employees who would leave quickly, as against those who would be likely to stay. However, it must be pointed out that this evidence applies to the United States in a very different economic climate from now, and involves a very complicated procedure.

One reason why many selectors shy away from the use of interest questionnaires is that, on the face of it, they appear to be very easy to fake. This is probably a very healthy caution. For example, if the questionnaire is being used for selection of sales people, it is easy for the applicant to see what required responses would show a stronger interest in things concerning the activity of selling. Or, if a KPR was being used in the selection of an office manager, the applicant might well feel that he would enhance his chances if he favoured the computational, persuasive, and clerical activities. However, one investigation[11] which set out to examine this issue of faking, hypothesized that, if people in a group responded to the SVIB when it was being used to select them in the same way as they responded when it was being used simply to help them in receiving vocational guidance, then that would be evidence that faking did not occur. The results supported the hypothesis. This therefore provides some evidence that people do not actually fake interest questionnaires, but the fact remains that it is possible and, more seriously, undetectable. This renders the device a dubious instrument for selection.

An important distinction between the measurement of interest and the measurement of ability lies in the area of standardization. As we have discussed, the aptitude test scores of applicants need to be compared with the scores of 'applicants in general'. In the case of interests, this can be very misleading, a point which is central in the development of one of the more recent British interest questionnaires.[12] Within the interest patterns of school-leavers, an enthusiasm for manual, computational and clerical activities does not feature particularly strongly. An individual who has, therefore, a moderate interest in these activities may find that these are identified as his strongest interests, relative to others of his age. If his claimed strongest interest was in 'helping people', which also happens to be a strong interest of others, it becomes devalued in his case. His real interest profile becomes distorted when expressed in relative terms – a distortion which would succeed in altering the 'facts'. This is, therefore, yet another danger for the selector in the use of interest measurements.

The nature and measurement of personality

Of all candidates' attributes, the one that indicates the greatest distinction between popular usage and psychological usage is that of personality. Recruiters have been heard to refer to it in its show-business sense, with the ideal candidate having 'bags of it'. Or it is sometimes used as a generic term to describe all candidates attributes other than attainment, which do or do not fit the job. An example would be the following comment by a selector 'He seems a very good candidate as he has good qualifications and the right personality to do the job'. Psychologists, especially those who are interested in why individuals differ one from another, pay particular attention to personality, but the common usage of the word is too broad. However, as with intelligence, there are many different definitions as to the nature of personality.

The differences are manifestations of the particular theoretical standpoint of the psychologist, although most of the theoretical approaches would accept the definition of personality as being 'characteristic patterns of behaviour and modes of thinking that determine a person's adjustment to the environment'[13] as an acceptable baseline. The importance of this definition is that the term 'characteristic' is meant to imply consistency.

Thus it could be said that psychologists do see personality as being about those enduring aspects of individuals which cause them to be different from other individuals. While a summary list of the theoretical approaches to personality would be 'trait', 'psychoanalytic', 'phenomenological', and 'learning', it is to the first of these that attention must be given. It is the 'trait' approach to personality that is most frequently referred to in the context of recruitment and selection. This is, however, not to dismiss the other approaches, but they are infrequently used and undeveloped for recruitment and selection purposes. To consider them would be both intriguing and challenging, but not in this text.

The trait approach
This embraces the idea of the personality type, that is, an all-embracing unique dimensional difference. For example, all individuals are on an introversion/extroversion dimension and personality differences can be described in terms of where individuals come on a scale which measures this. The idea of personality traits is that personality does not refer to an all-embracing difference, but to a whole range of characteristics, thus offering a multi-dimensional model. Theorists differ quite significantly, however, on the number of traits that exist. Some will argue that there

are only two or three identifiable, enduring and independent traits. Whereas others will claim that it is possible to identify as many as sixteen or twenty of them.

The value of this approach to the selector is self-apparent. If a job requires that the incumbent possesses certain traits, then selection is about identifying these. It may be felt that a job requires the individual to be extroverted rather than introverted, assertive rather than compliant, low rather than high in anxiety. These could be seen as three personality traits and the selection procedure contains attempts to identify the extent to which these exist in candidates.

This, however, does raise problems. Apart from knowing if they really are important in job performance, there is the question of how we recognize them in a candidate, and what about other traits? Three have been identified as important, but does that mean that if there are others they do not matter? Both these points are tied up in the problems of measurement.

The measurement of personality

In practice, the most common method of measuring personality in selection is by observation. It is during the interview that most judgements concerning this aspect of the candidate are made. The reason why the trait approach has been more influential than other approaches is the convenience of it to the interviewer as a personality assessment method. It is also the approach to personality which has propagated attempts at objective measurement. The use of standardized personality measures (which, like the measurement of interest, should not be referred to as 'personality tests' because of the need to avoid the idea of a pass/fail cut off point) is referred to as 'personality questionnaires' or 'personality inventories'.

Personality inventories normally depend on self-observation. It is a questionnaire in which a person reports reactions or feelings in certain situations. There are broadly two approaches. Firstly, there are those based on trait theory models, emanating from certain personality theorists who have identified the existence of a finite number of personality traits. This has usually been done by using a multivariate statistical method such as factor analysis. A large number of draft situational questions are presented to large samples of individuals and are analysed to elicit any independent factors. The most widely used inventory of this type in the UK is Cattell's 16PF.

Secondly, there are the empirically constructed personality inventories. Two examples of these are the Minnesota Multiphase Personality Inventory (MMPI) and the California Psychological Inventory (CPI). Instead of assuming specific personality traits and formulating questions to measure them, hundreds of test questions are given to groups of individuals, each group being known to differ from the norm on a particular criterion. In the case of the MMPI, the criterion groups are those who have been clinically diagnosed to be suffering from some personality defect, that is some sort of psychological disorder. In the case of the CPI, the criterion groups are those, not necessary clinically diagnosed, rated as extremes in terms of traits by their peers. Thus, in the design of these inventories, those questions that discriminate between the normal groups and the criterion groups are retained to form the questions of the inventory.

As with interest inventories, there are problems with personality inventories. They rely on an individual's ability to understand the question and his or her willingness to answer honestly. Also, in personality inventories, there is often an easily identified best answer, that is the most socially acceptable answer. This therefore allows for a tendency to answer in the direction of job requirements. In addition to this, as many inventories require the answer 'yes' or 'no', there is a problem of acquiescence, that is the tendency to answer 'yes' rather than 'no'.

Attempts have been made in the design of inventories to reduce faking statistically by the use of 'lie scales', but these are not very effective at identifying deliberate lying. A further problem with standardized personality measurements is the interpretation of the inventory scores. Devices such as Cattell's 16PF produce the candidate scores on a large number of traits. Some of these traits are recognizable as being relevant to job performance, but not necessarily all of them. Therefore should the apparently non-relevant ones be discounted? An extreme example of this problem is where an organization was only interested in the score on one trait. Using a 16PF, it therefore totally ignored the remaining fifteen. In terms of the individual who was to be employed, this would be flying in the face of the psychological basis of the measuring device.

The way round the problem is to match the whole personality profile with the job. This can often only be done by inspection – a very subjective activity which can mitigate against any objective quality claimed for the personality measuring device.

The difficulty in using a questionnaire like the 16PF is that it has been designed as a general personality measure, and not specifically developed for employee selection. This can cause it to be unacceptable to selectors seeking a standardized, objective personality measure and, if used, can produce interpretation difficulties as mentioned above. The Occupational Personality Questionnaire (OPQ) has been developed in Britain in the 1980s. It is a derivative of the 16PF which is intended specifically to be used in occupational settings such as selection. It benefits from this focus but there still remains the ultimate interpretation problems referred to above.

The usefulness of personality measurement in selection is not without its critics. Recently two validity issues have been raised. The first of these concerns the inherent structure of the questionnaire used. Some measures, such as those that are versions of the time-honoured DISC system, consist of a small number of dimensions of personality which are 'shared out' within anyone completing the questionnaire.[14] For example, a high score on any one dimension must be compensated by a lowering of scores on one or more of the other dimensions. The total when all the scores for an individual are added together will always be the same for everyone. These are referred to as 'ipsative' measures and change the scale property of the dimension from 'interval' to 'ordinal' (see Chapter 3). For this reason, as the dimensions are interdependent, it has been argued that such measures cannot be used in selection if there is any attempt to compare candidates on these individual dimensions.[15] Not only do they have no psychological meaning on their own, but they have no statistical meaning either, and therefore no validity.

Whilst this has caused some debate amongst psychologists[16] it is probably safer to use ipsative measures only by taking overviews of total profiles obtained by individuals on the questionnaire when comparing them as candidates in selection.

The second validity issue concerns non-ipsative personality measures that consist of large numbers of dimensions (e.g. CPI, 16PF, OPQ). A case has been made that questionnaires using these numbers will appear more valid than they really are. This is because, in validity studies, high correlation coefficients (again see Chapter 3) may occur by chance.[17]

Clearly this criticism would be well founded if producers of questionnaires were to use the output of such studies carelessly or dishonestly. It is not, however, reason to write off the value of personality measurement. It is a statistical debate that loses sight of the underlying principle of personality assessment. Any measure can be deemed to have validity if it is possible to demonstrate, in objective terms, that it improves a selector's level of understanding, which in turn allows proper discrimination between candidates to take place. This may include methods that rely on feeding back the questionnaire results to candidates for their comment before judgements are made.

Compared with interests, personality characteristics are more occupationally relevant. It would be both unwise and indeed dangerous if an organization was to recruit a manager who consistently approached his leadership function in an assertive and authoritarian way, if the organizational climate in which he or she was to operate demanded a much more democratic approach. Having identified that this was a characteristic which the job required, the information could be elicited from the candidates through the selection of the application form describing previous jobs, from references which might refer to this characteristic, from the interview where experience and interests can be investigated and behaviour actually observed, or from some standardized measuring technique. In other words, the value of the concepts of personality, especially those offered by the trait theorists, is in terms of what the selector ought to be looking for. Some traits do appear to be useful in selection.[18] The actual methods of unearthing these traits, which these theorists and other psychologists put forward, are probably less helpful. Some other, more esoteric, methods are discussed briefly in Chapter 10.

This chapter has dealt as some length with the psychological attributes of candidates. As we have seen, questions such as 'How do we understand them and measure them?' have not been totally answered by psychologists. The psychologists' role is more concerned with asking the questions rather than answering them. Recruiters do not have to be trained psychologists in order to handle human attributes in selection, but perhaps they do have to take note of psychological methodology and the caveats issued. If these are ignored, then there is a danger that there will be yet another attempt to re-invent the wheel. The world of psychology may not deliver the answers, but it has spent a lot of time thinking through some of the problems.

Summary

Selection involves the assessment of psychological attributes. It concerns itself with the nature and measurement of ability, which includes attainment, aptitude, and competence. Theoretical models have been developed to explain the structure of abilities and these have strongly influenced the types of psychological tests which are produced. The nature and measurement of interest and personality are crucial issues.

Selectors, while they do not need to be trained psychologists, do need to have some understanding of what psychologists have to say. Psychological attributes of candidates cannot be successfully assessed without this appreciation.

References

1 P. E. Vernon, *Intelligence: Heredity and Environment* (San Francisco: W. H. Freeman 1979).

2 S. J. Closs, *Manual of the APU Interest Guide* (Hodder & Stoughton 1975).

3 P. E. Vernon, *The Structure of Human Abilities* (Methuen 1950).

4 J. P. Guilford, *The Nature of Human Intelligence* (McGraw-Hill 1967).

5 L. Tyler, *Individuality* (Jossey-Bass, San Francisco 1978).

6 L. L. Thurstone, 'Primary Mental Abilities', *Psychometric Monograph no. 1* (University of Chicago Press 1943).

7 S. Downs, 'Trainability testing', *The Recruitment Handbook*, 3rd ed., D. Ungerson (ed.) (Gower Press 1983).

8 K. Pearlman, F. L. Schmidt and J. E. Hunter, 'Validity generalisation results for tests used to predict training success and job proficiency in clerical occupations', *Journal of Applied Psychology,* **65** (1980), p. 373–406.

9 M. L. Tenopyr, 'The realities of employment testing', *American Psychologist,* **36** (1981), no. 10, p. 1120–7.

10 J. Tiffin and R. F. Phelan, 'Use of the Kuder Preference Record to predict turnover in an industrial plant', *Personnel Psychology,* **6** (1953), 195–204.

11 N. M. Abrahams, I. Neumann and W. H. Gilthens, 'Faking vocational interests: simulated versus real life motivation', *Personnel Psychology,* **24** (1971), p. 5–12.

12 Closs, *Manual of the APU Interest Guide.*

13 E. R. Hilgard, R. C. Atkinson and R. L. Atkinson, *Introduction to Psychology,* 7th ed. (Harcourt Brace & Jovanovich 1980).

14 W. M. Marston, Emotions of Normal People (Harcourt Brace 1928).

15 C. E. Johnson, R. Wood and S. F. Blinkhorn, 'Spuriouser and spuriouser: The use of ipsative personality tests'; *Journal of Occupational Psychology,* **61** (1988), p. 153–62.

16 S. B. Blinkhorn and C. Johnson, 'The insignificance of personality testing', *Nature,* **348** (December 1990), p. 671–2.

17 P. Saville and E. Wilson, 'The reliability and the validity of normative and ipsative approaches in the measurement of personality', *Journal of Occupational Psychology,* **64** (1991), p. 219–38.

18 M. R. Barrick and M. K. Mount, 'The big five personality dimensions and job performance: a meta-analysis', *Personnel Psychology,* **44** (1991), p. 1–26.

5
The right to select versus the ability to select

What has been considered in previous chapters has been the nature of the attributes of candidates and methods of measuring these. This has been done ignoring any constraints that might be externally imposed upon the selector, or indeed the recruiter. It is now necessary to consider these.

If an organization wishes to recruit and select people, it is, of course, in its own interests to have the ability to carry it out successfully. But, by and large, this is a problem which is internal to the organization. In other words, as far as Great Britain is concerned, an organization almost has the right to select or reject who it wants. If it does it badly or unfairly, it is the concern of the organization. Relative to other countries, for example the United States, there are very few legal constraints in the area of recruitment and selection.

This can often come as a surprise to failed candidates who pursue an explanation for their failure, especially if they feel this is related to such attributes as qualifications, age or handicap.

Having stated this, an organization does not, however, have an absolute right to select who it wishes. The law does have something very definite to say about it.

In addition to the legal aspects, there are, of course, ethical consider-ations. These can be internal constraints within the organization, or indeed within the recruiters or selectors themselves. Or they can be external, in as much as that wider public opinion could turn against the organization if they are ignored.

One of the features of selection in the 1980s is the growing acceptance that it should be fair and equitable – the legislation of the mid-1970s appears to have struck home. A reason for this is that continued high unemployment has meant more dissatisfied job applicants; thus the fairness of selection methods has been under closer scrutiny.[1]

The legal aspects

The most direct legal intervention in the recruitment and selection process is in the area of discrimination. Firstly with regard to sex, and secondly with regard to race.

Sex discrimination

Under the Sex Discrimination Act of 1975 the Equal Opportunities Commission was set up. This body has the duty of eliminating discrimination at all levels and in every field with regard to sex.[2] While the Act is primarily directed towards the protection of women, it applies equally to men; and also to 'married persons' as distinct from 'single persons'. For the sake of clarity, it will be discussed below with reference to discrimination against 'women'.

There are two kinds of discrimination, 'direct' and 'indirect'. In recruitment and selection 'direct' discrimination arises where a prospective employer treats a woman less favourably than he would treat a man, on the grounds of sex. For this to be established, note is taken of what is said, or what can be inferred from all the circumstances surrounding the case. 'Indirect' discrimination occurs when a selection requirement is applied to both sexes but the ability of one sex to comply with it is considerably smaller than that of the other and cannot be justified. If an organization recruiting computer programmers stipulated that they must be over six feet tall, such an irrelevant condition would be discriminatory and unjustifiable as women would be far less likely to be able to comply with the requirement. In such a case, any action can only be brought by a complainant who cannot comply with the conditions.

Whilst the *intention* to discriminate is an important issue with regard to the broad area of rights and abilities in selection, it is not the concern of the Act. The test is not to find an *intention* to discriminate but whether the *effect* is to discriminate. To establish whether there is discrimination, a comparison must be made with persons of the opposite sex whose relevant circumstances are the same or not materially different.

Discrimination against *married persons* and victimization of persons who have brought proceedings or given evidence under the Acts is also outlawed.

It is therefore unlawful in establishments in Great Britain in recruitment and selection to discriminate against a person on the grounds of sex or marital status, firstly in terms of the actual recruitment and selection process by deliberately seeking to take on only men or women or single persons, or by refusing or deliberately omitting to offer employment on the grounds of sex or marital status, and secondly in terms of the conditions of service offered to successful candidates.

Following the passing of the Act in 1975, there was a spate of bizarre attempts to get around it, for example the case of the publican who, when prevented from advertising for barmaids, sought 'bar staff who are willing to work in low cut dresses'. Many of these failed to recognize that it was equally unlawful to make conditions which might result in an act of discrimination. However any Act such as this requires exceptions to make it workable. It does not apply to the armed services and ministers of religion, and there are certain occupational qualifications which, if genuine, make discrimination lawful. These have been summarized as follows:[3]

1 Physiological reasons – these do *not* include strength and stamina but other reasons. An example would be the recruitment of a model for women's clothing.

2 Privacy or decency – jobs which require physical contact with, or working with, people who are undressed, for example baths and lavatory attendants.

3 Accommodation – where there exist sleeping and sanitary facilities for only one sex and it is *unreasonable* to expect the employer to make extra provision.

4 Character of the establishment – one sex is appropriate because of the basis character of the establishment, for example prison warders.

5 Education and welfare – where personal service promoting welfare or education can best be provided by members of only one sex, then discrimination is possible. An example of this would be the appointment of house masters in boys' boarding schools.

6 Statutory bar – this relates to the restrictions of statute, mainly the Factories Act which does not permit women to be employed in certain categories.

7 Married couples – the Act permits discrimination against wives or legal discrimination in their favour because of the particular employment circumstances of the husband.

8 Overseas working – where a job involves working overseas in a country where the laws and customs are such that the work could not be performed by a woman, it would not be unlawful to discriminate against them.

To give examples to illustrate all the aspects of the Sex Discrimination Act would, of course, take up a great deal of space. What is important for those involved in recruitment and selection is to empathize with the spirit of the Act especially as this would avoid the rather transparent attempts that have occurred in the past to try to get round it. Selection interviewers often make heavy weather of trying to avoid falling foul of the Act in the questions that they put to candidates. An example of interviewing practice which the Act is clearly designed to outlaw is asking young women applicants about their marital plans, including any intention about having children, questions which male applicants for similar jobs are never asked. The Act quite simply classifies this as discriminatory since men and women are not being treated equally. Further, it has been ruled that asking both men and women the same question may still be illegal. Questions concerning intentions about having children have a different significance to women than they do for men (*Morley v. London Borough of Bexley, 1985*).

The value of the Act is that instead of interviewers therefore mechanically posing the same questions to the male applicant, it encourages them to consider why this area is in fact being investigated at all. If, for example, it is a concern related to the future geographical mobility of the employee, then the simple legal and logical alternative would be to ask applicants of both sexes to say how they feel about the future prospect that the job would require some postings to different geographical locations.

For illustrations of the workings of the Sex Discrimination Act in relation to recruitment, see Examples 5.1 and 5.2. The first of these illustrates that, while discrimination by age is not in itself illegal, the imposing of age limits in recruitment and selection can sometimes be deemed as indirect discrimination.[4]

Example 5.1

A woman applied for employment in the Executive grade of the Civil Service but her application was refused on the grounds that she was over the age limit of 28 for first entry. After failing with a complaint to a Tribunal she appealed to the Employment Appeal Tribunal, claiming that few women could meet the age limit as it was set at an age when many women were having babies and looking after children. The finding was in her favour. (*Price v. Civil Service Commission and Society of Civil and Public Servants, 1976*)

Example 5.2

A woman and her husband were employed by the same company and the woman was not considered for a more senior position because her husband was a subordinate of the person for whom she would be working. It was held that this discrimination was not unlawful. (*Martin v. National Car Parks, 1976*)

A point worth adding on the topic of sexual discrimination is that a frequently cited 'rationale' for this discrimination is that men and women seek different things from their work, and they should therefore be treated differently in selection. This view results from the practice of comparing how women in jobs largely performed by women see their work with how men in jobs largely performed by men see theirs. If, however, women and men in the same jobs are compared, the difference between what each sex is seeking largely disappears.[5]

Under the Sex Discrimination Act 1986 amendments were made to the 1975 Act which have implications for selection. Firstly, private households and undertakings of five employees or fewer, excluded under the first Act, became no longer exempt. Secondly, some of the statutory bars were removed.

Race discrimination

The law relating to racial discrimination is almost identical to that relating to sex discrimination. The Race Relations Act of 1976 set up the Commission for Racial Equality which, like the Equal Opportunities Commission, is given the duty of eliminating discrimination at all levels and in every field. As with the Sex Discrimination Act there are two kinds of discrimination, *direct* and *indirect*. Against it does not matter, under the Act, whether there is *intention* to discriminate. It is unlawful if the *effect* is to discriminate. There can also be discrimination by victimization. It is unlawful, therefore, in establishments in Great Britain in recruitment and selection to discriminate against a person by, firstly, setting out not to offer employment to members of certain racial groups, or to refuse or deliberately omit to offer employment on the grounds of race. Or, secondly, to offer different conditions of employment to members of different racial groups.

As with sex discrimination, it is unlawful to make a requirement or condition which results in an act of discrimination. There are exceptions to the Act where race is a genuine *occupational qualification*. These are less numerous than with sex discrimination and are:

1 Entertainment – where authentic presentation requires a person from a particular racial group.

2 Artistic or photographic modelling for similar reasons as 1.

3 Specialized restaurants – where food and drink is served to the public in a special setting it may be necessary to have a person from a particular racial group in order to sustain that setting.

4 Community social workers – personal services to members of a particular racial group may best be provided by someone within that racial group.

It is again useful for those in recruitment and selection to appreciate the spirit of the 1976 Race Relations Act. There is, however, a suspicion that some organizations have tried to get round the Act in some way by, for example, requesting applicants to send a photograph with their application form. If there are large numbers of applicants, it allows the organization to preselect or screen out members of ethnic groups before they are invited to interview, thus preventing the interviewer from falling foul of the Act. Organizations which have attempted this devious practice have failed to recognize that, if a disproportionately large number of applicants from an ethnic group were failing to get to the interview stage of the selection, then the organization would be seen to be blatantly guilty of discrimination, as they have in their possession a lot of information concerning applicants of ethnic origin.

For illustrations of the operation of the Act see the cases presented in Examples 5.3 and 5.4.

Example 5.3

A tractor manufacturer employed only a tiny number of black workers, despite its location in the Coventry area. The reason for this was the firm's reliance on unsolicited letters of application for jobs. However, when vacancies occurred these letters were examined and candidates short-listed. The firm gave preference to those who submitted a letter of application in good English, those who specified their experience, qualifications and the type of work they wanted, and those who applied at the time a suitable vacancy appeared. This was held to be indirect discrimination, as it gave a clear advantage to those who could find out about the firm's recruitment and vacancies from existing employees. Because nearly all the existing employees were white, and because they tended to give such information to other white people, the effect of this method of recruitment was to exclude black applicants. (*Massey Ferguson Perkins Ltd – Report of a Formal Investigation* – Commission for Racial Equality 1982)

Example 5.4

An orthodox Sikh who wore a beard which was required by his religion applied for a job in a chocolate factory. He was refused because the prospective employer applied a strict rule of no beards or excessively long hair on the grounds of hygiene. Following a complaint of indirect discrimination, it was asserted that the rule was justifiable. It was held that, as there was scientific evidence to support the employer's contention, there was no discrimination. (*Panesar v. The Nestle Co. Ltd, 1980*)[6]

A more recent development in the prevention of racial discrimination has been the Code of Practice of the Commission for Racial Equality. This came into force in April 1984.[7] A year later a similar Code of Practice produced by the Equal Opportunities Commission was seen.

The aim of the Code is to give practical guidance to employers, and others, to help them understand the provisions of the 1976 Race Relations Act and their implications. Its aim is also to help employers implement policies to eliminate racial discrimination and enhance equal opportunities.

The status of this Code should be noted. While it 'does not impose any legal obligations itself, nor is it an authoritative statement of the Law ... its provisions are admissible in evidence in any proceedings under the Race Relations Act before an Industrial Tribunal and if any provision appears to the Tribunal to be relevant to a question arising in the proceedings it must be taken into account in determining that question'.[8]

Organizations, therefore, would be well advised to take heed of the recommendations of the Code. If it can be demonstrated, for example, that the steps set out in the Code have been taken to prevent employees from committing acts of unlawful discrimination, then liability for such acts may be avoided in any legal proceedings brought against the employers. Obviously, failure to take the steps may incur liability.

The Code is of real value to those involved in selection as it can prevent unintentional, but nevertheless discriminatory, illegal selection practices – remembering that individual selection decision-makers have a great deal of opportunity to break the law.

Probably the most controversial aspect of the Code is the recommendation that the ethnic origin of a workforce be recorded. This also includes all job applicants.[9] As far as the selector is concerned, this has serious implications for the design of application forms and will therefore be discussed in Chapter 10.

Other recommendations which have a bearing on recruitment and selection are given below. They should be borne in mind when reading some of the later chapters of this book.

In *recruitment* the recommendations are that:

- Employers should not confine advertisements unjustifiably to those areas or publications which would exclude or disproportionately reduce the numbers of applicants of a particular racial group.

- Employers should avoid prescribing requirements such as length of residence or experience in the UK, and where a particular qualification is required it should be made clear that a fully comparable qualification obtained overseas is as acceptable as a UK qualification.

- Employers should not confine recruitment unjustifiably to those agencies, job centres, careers offices and schools which, because of their particular source of applicants, provide only or mainly applicants of a particular racial group.

- It should not solely, or in the first instance, be through the recommendation of existing employees, where the workforce concerned is wholly or predominantly white or black and the labour market is multi-racial.

- It should not be through procedures by which applicants are mainly or wholly supplied through trade unions, where this means that only members of a particular racial group, or a disproportionately high number of them come forward.

In *selection* the recommendations are that:

- Selection criteria and tests are examined to ensure that they are related to job requirements and are not unlawfully discriminatory. (For example, applicants should not be disqualified because they are unable to complete an application form unassisted unless personal completion of the form is a valid test of the standard of English required for the safe and effective performance of the job.)

- Gate, reception and personnel staff should be instructed, in writing, not to treat casual or formal applications from particular racial groups less favourably than others.

- Staff responsible for shortlisting, interviewing and selecting candidates should be:
  a   clearly informed of selection criteria and of the need for their consistent application
  b   given guidance and training on the effects which generalized assumptions and prejudices about race can have on selection decisions
  c   made aware of the possible misunderstandings that can occur in interviews between persons of different cultural backgrounds.
  Whatever possible, shortlisting and interviewing should not be done by one person alone, but should at least be checked at a more senior level.

Adherence to all the above recommendations is not always easy, but at least a valid reason should be at hand to justify those found to be difficult.

The two major pieces of legislation which we have been considering, along with the Factories Act, are the only legal interventions in the work of the recruiter and selector in Great Britain. The picture in the United States is somewhat different, and it is perhaps worth dwelling on this for a while, as it could be argued that, as their equal employment opportunity legislation predates our own, the American situation is therefore more developed, and may provide a glimpse into the future.

Equal Employment Opportunity and the law in the United States
The Equal Employment Opportunity laws make it illegal to indicate a preference in recruitment on the grounds of sex, age, race, colour, religion or national origin, but in addition to this there are many State anti-discrimination laws, for example those carrying out selection in the State of New York must not, either on application forms or during the interview, do the following:

1 Enquire of a woman's ability to reproduce and attitude towards family planning.

2 Require a photograph of an applicant at any time before hiring.

3 Enquire about religious affiliation.

4 Ask age, or date of birth, but it is legal to ask whether the person is between the ages of 18 and 70.[10]

The Federal Administration of Equal Employment Opportunities legislation is the responsibility of the Equal Employment Opportunities Commission (EEOC). With regard to the candidates' attributes, this body has ruled that education and training requirements must have a manifest relationship to the jobs for which people are being hired. Thus, seeking a graduate with an unspecified degree for a position could be deemed to be illegal.[11] It is in the area of selection testing that the influence of the EEOC makes the American situation very different from that in Great Britain.

The EEOC has issued guidelines which require that selection tests are properly validated. This must be carried out by the collection of job performance data and the correlation of such data statistically with test scores for a representative sample of people.[12] The placing of the onus on the employer to demonstrate statistically that a selection test does not unfairly discriminate against certain groups, rather than on the employee to demonstrate that he or she has been discriminated against, is a result largely of two important cases in the US Supreme Court. These cases – namely *Griggs* v. *Duke Power Company, 1971*, and the *Arbarmall Paper Company* v. *Moody, 1975* – were both instances where black employees challenged the use of standardized tests and the companies were unable to provide valid statistical data to demonstrate that the tests did not discriminate. As a result of the high standards for testing that the EEOC and the Courts have imposed, many companies have abandoned them. They feel that it is just not worthwhile investing effort in developing a testing programme to meet such rigorous standards. The irony of the situation is that it has meant a movement towards other selection methods which are actually less easy to validate, for example, the interview. Federal 'Guidelines' have urged employers to seek alternative selection procedures which are equally valid but have less adverse effects on minorities. But one study has indicated that this request may be difficult to meet.[13] It has provided evidence that only biographical data and peer evaluation produce results valid enough to equate with those of standardized tests. It found it difficult to produce any evidence that other selection procedures could match the validity of tests.

At present, therefore, there seems to be, under current United States employment law, a contradiction. Selection tests, while having the highest demonstrable predictive validity, are the principal villains of unfairly discriminatory selection. A Special Committee set up by the US National Research Council to examine the practice of ability testing argued that it is not the tests themselves which are responsible for the effects against disadvantaged groups, but the way in which they are used. The report of that Committee advocated that tests should not be used by themselves, but in conjunction with other sources of information.[14]

A final point concerning equitable selection in the United States relates to the rather dubious practice of pre-employment genetic screening. It has been reported[15] that it is being applied on a limited scale by some companies to weed out job applicants whose 'genetic defects' might increase their occupational health risk upon exposure to certain substances used in the workplace. The justification for its use has been the protection of the employee. The practice must give grounds for concern as it leaves the door wide open for abuse. Surely, when evidence is produced that aspects of the job are dangerous to certain types of employee, then it is the job that needs changing.

Ethical considerations

It is obviously very difficult to list what an organization's ethical considerations should be. Clearly discrimination on the grounds of sex, or race, is deemed unethical, but, as we have already seen, the law takes care of these. Two areas, however, where it has very little to say are those concerning age and handicap.

As we have seen, age can be a dominant feature in cases of indirect sexual discrimination, but usually, as far as the law is concerned, that is the end of it. However, discrimination on the grounds of age, in practice, is the source of a great deal of anxiety amongst candidates, especially at a time when many people are finding themselves thrown out of jobs because of redundancy in mid-career. From a candidate's point of view, it may be seen as unfortunate that the imposing of upper age limits in recruitment and selection is often determined not by job performance needs but by the rules of pension funds, and it is indeed a difficult pill to swallow for the 46 year old candidate who is informed that the maximum age for employment in the organization is 45 because the pension fund cannot accept new members above that age.

The other disadvantaged group is the handicapped or disabled. They, of course, do have some protection from the law in as much as that it requires that at least 3 per cent of employees of each organization employing more than twenty workers should be registered as disabled. While this does enhance the employment prospect of the handicapped and disabled, it is not necessarily the type of help they really need. It is seen as a form of positive discrimination which highlights their difference from the rest of the workforce, a difference which is often irrelevant to job performance and one that members of that particular group feel employers should ignore rather than enhance.

One of the effects of the advent of high technology, especially in the area of computer controlled activities, is that jobs which formerly had a high manual content and were therefore unsuitable for many disabled people, have now become much more easily manageable for them. An ethical consideration, therefore, is that those involved in recruitment and selection recognize this.

A further ethical problem is best illustrated by a question which was recently posed to the author. It was simply 'How soon will it be before graduate recruitment becomes illegal?' Whilst this may, at first, seem a rather strange question, it does highlight the fact that in graduate recruitment you have a situation where a large section of the population is prevented from applying for certain jobs in organizations because they do not possess a university or polytechnic degree. Yet it might be very difficult for the employing organization to demonstrate that the possession of that degree was necessary for the candidate to perform the job of the graduate recruit. In terms of 'fairness', the degree as a valid measure of aptitude for managerial responsibility should be demonstrated. It is worth noting, as we have discussed, that the EEOC in the United States has already devoted its attention to this issue.

The example of graduate recruitment is, of course, just one that relates to discrimination on the grounds of formal qualification. Whether those involved in recruitment and selection should give heed to ethical considerations over and above those related to the law has to be, in the end, a matter of individual conscience, or the extent to which such considerations are of value from a public relations viewpoint.

Unintentional discrimination

Most of the constraints on the right to select are concerned specifically with the idea of unfair discrimination. As we have discussed, if this constraint is a legal one it is of no concern whether the discrimination is intentional or not. This may seem to those involved in recruitment and selection to be a little harsh. The argument could be made that if an organization sets out, for example, to intentionally disadvantage women in recruitment terms, this must not be allowed to happen, but if the organization has no intention but it just 'works out that way', then that is a different story. It is therefore important at this stage to point out that when unintentional discrimination does occur it is often the result of using selection devices, the effect of which has not been sufficiently closely scrutinized.

One way in which this type of discrimination can occur was highlighted some time ago[16] and was shown to be related to the nature of the group of people from whom an organization is recruiting. It is often assumed in recruitment and selection that once the group to be selected from is identified then it can be assumed that that group is homogenous in character; for example, a company wishing to recruit typists between the ages of 18 and 21 in Central London assumes that, as a group, the candidates are relatively similar, the only differences being in relation to their skills as typists. The selection procedure should try to identify the differences in these skills so that the best candidate can be selected. This fails to recognize that many such groups contain sub-groups which are different from one another. In other words, the pool of people from which we are selecting the typist is not homogenous but in fact hetero-geneous, containing groups identified by racial origin, socio-economic level, and sex. The assumption of homogenity may have led an organiza-tion to very carefully validate a selection test. However, what it was totally unaware of was that any apparent validity was being caused by different test performances by members of different groups. The situation is illustrated in Figure 7.

The organization had applicants from both boys and girls. On average, girls did better on the selection test, and indeed turned out to be better typists than boys, who did less well on the test and turned out to be less able typists. Even though for each of these groups the test was totally invalid, when the two groups were combined it gave an appearance of validity which was totally spurious. In fact to use such a test in selection was totally discriminatory against the boys.

It would be unlikely, however, that in such a case as this, an organization would be aware of the unfair discriminatory nature of the selection method it was using, especially as it had gone through a validation procedure which the organization felt was a very responsible thing to do.

A note of caution – discrimination through a failure to recognize the existence of racial sub-groups has been highlighed by research largely emanating from the United States – indeed the evidence has strongly influenced the guidelines issued by the Equal Employment Opportunities Commission.[17] While it remains a very important issue, much of this work has been challenged on the grounds that serious sampling errors have occurred in assessing test validities for minority groups. Results of studies have suggested that, if these errors are corrected, single group validity by race does not occur any more frequently than by chance.[18] This has provoked the following comment: 'The research findings of the

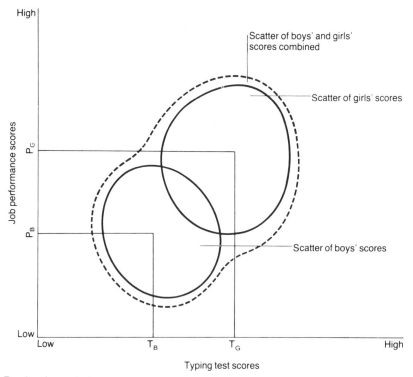

High

Scatter of boys' and girls' scores combined

Scatter of girls' scores

Job performance scores

P_G

P_B

Scatter of boys' scores

Low

Low T_B T_G High

Typing test scores

T_B = boys' mean test score
T_G = girls' mean test score
P_B = boys' mean performance score
P_G = girls' mean performance score

Figure 7 *Spurious test validity resulting from the combination of sub-groups for which the test has no validity*

1970s show that we can no longer entertain the belief that the problem is in the tests and that it can be solved by modifying or eliminating the tests. Instead we must face the problem, which is that some groups of individuals are not acquiring the cognitive skills needs in modern society to the same degree as others, and we must focus on ways of improving acquisition of these skills.[19]

This chapter, in focusing on the right versus the ability to select, has devoted much attention to constraints on the right to select. This is because the rest of the book is devoted to enhancing the ability to select. The American experience has been that the two are, of course, interrelated. As the employer's rights to select are restricted, so there is a need for him to improve his ability, not just for the sake of getting the right person for the right job, but in order to justify the equity of his procedures, though it will, nevertheless, enhance the quality of his selection decisions. Because of the relatively powerful rights of the recruiter and selector in Britain, the subsequent level of ability is that much less. This is best illustrated by the selector who takes great pride in his equitable approach to candidates by telling those who have failed why they have not been successful. However, in practice this information is often couched in terms of vague generalizations, comparing one candidate with the others, and including some well-meaning potted careers guidance, instead of specific attributes on which the candidate might in future work. This is because the selector has exercised his right to make a selection decision, the detailed explanation of which might reveal a distinct lack of ability.

Summary

In Britain, unlike, for example, the United States, the employer can select or reject any applicant almost at will. These are some legal restrictions which are aimed at preventing unfair discrimination, namely the Sex Discrimination Act (1975) and the Race Relations Act (1976). An important feature of both Acts is that intent is not an issue. Unintentional discrimination can occur which is nevertheless illegal. The Commission for Racial Equality has introduced a Code of Practice to go some way to help avoid this. Ethical constraints, especially with regard to age, and physical or mental handicap, should not be ignored. It might be a short-sighted policy for an organization to consider legal obligations only.

There is some evidence that the focus is moving from the 'right' to select to the 'ability' to select.

References

1 C. Lewis, 'What's new in selection', *Personnel Management* (January 1984), p. 14–16.
2 C. Waud, *Redundancy and Unfair Dismissal 1982–1983* (Harmsworth 1983).
3 D. Torrington and J. Chapman, *Personnel Management*, 2nd ed. (Prentice-Hall 1983).
4 Waud, *Redundancy and Unfair Dismissal*.
5 K. G. Wheeler, 'Sex differences in perceptions of desired rewards, availability of rewards and abilities in relation to occupational selection', *Journal of Occupational Psychology*, **54** (1981).
6 Waud, *Redundancy and Unfair Dismissal*.
7 'Code of Practice for the elimination of racial discrimination and the promotion of equality of opportunity in employment', Commission for Racial Equality, London (July 1983).
8 *ibid.*
9 P. Crofts, 'Concentrating on monitoring for racial equality', *Personnel Management* (March 1984), p. 26–30.
10 Rulings on Inquiries Relating to Race, Creed, Color, National Origin, Sex, Age,

Disability, Marital Status, and Arrest Record (Albany: State of New York, Division of Human Rights 1975).

11 EEOC Decision No. 70–402 January – Labor Law Reports, Employment Practices Guide, vol. 1 (Chicago: Commerce Clearing House 1970).

12 D. S. Beach, *Personnel: The Management of People at Work* (Macmillan 1980).

13 R. R. Reilly and G. T. Chao, 'Validity of fairness of some alternative employee selection procedures', *Personnel Psychology*, **35** (1982).

14 A. K. Wigdor and W. R. Garner, *Ability Testing: Uses, consequences and controversies*, Part 1: Report of the Commission, National Research Council (Washington: National Academic Press 1982).

15 *International Management* (March 1983), p. 4.

16 C. J. Bartlett and B. S. O'Leary, 'A differential model to moderate the effect of heterogeneous groups in personnel selection and classification', *Personnel Psychology*, **22** (1969), p. 1–17.

17 J. Ledvinka, 'The statistical definition of fairness in the federal selection guidelines and its implications for minority employment', *Personnel Psychology*, **32** (1979), p. 551–62.

18 V. R. Boehm, 'Differential prediction: A methodological artifact?', *Journal of Applied Psychology*, **62** (1977), p. 146–54.
   J. E. Hunter and F. L. Schmidt, 'Differential and single group validity of employment tests by race: A critical analysis of three recent studies', *Journal of Applied Psychology*, **63** (1978), p. 1–11.

19 F. L. Schmidt and J. E. Hunter, 'Employment testing: Old theories and new research findings', *American Psychology*, **36** (1980), no. 10, p. 1128–37.

Section Two
Practices and Principles
of Selection

This section focuses on the practical aspects of selection rather than on the fundamental considerations underlying the process. It deals with such questions as: 'Who should do the recruitment and selection?'; 'Do they understand the job being recruited for?'; 'How will they attract sufficient applicants?'; 'How will they deal with the likely case of there being too many applicants?'; 'What methods of selection will they choose?'; 'What will they do with the information which these methods produce?'; and finally 'How will they know if it is working and if it has been worthwhile?'. Unlike Section One this section will be more concerned with 'How to do it'. However, this does not mean it is free from additional dilemmas and controversies.

6
Acquiring recruitment and selection staff

An organization, having made the decision to either solve or prevent a problem by the use of recruitment and selection, is faced with the initial task of acquiring the human resource to undertake this activity. The decision to operate this strategy assumes that the non-human resource implications have been taken care of. While this might be a little naïve, the skills of negotiating a larger recruitment and selection budget are outside the scope of this book.

The problem of who is going to do the recruitment and selection may seem to be of little importance unless an organization is starting from scratch, or is confronted with a sudden expansion of some magnitude. Many organizations will have a well-established personnel activity and it is assumed that therein lies a perfectly adequate human resource: be it a personnel department or, in the case of a small organization, a member of staff with a clearly identified executive responsibility for handling these matters. Indeed it is frequently the owner of the business himself who undertakes this work, if the size of the task permits. But ignoring its importance can be dangerous.

Firstly, in a stable economic climate, the staffing of such an activity will remain more or less constant, even though there may be marked peaks and troughs in recruitment and selection activity. If under-utilization is not to be permitted, there are going to be occasions when the recruitment and selection resource will need to be supplemented from elsewhere.

Secondly, those outside the personnel function, namely line managers, will inevitably intervene at some stage of the selection decision-making, albeit towards the end. The issue of acquiring recruitment and selection resources is much more than simply asking 'How do you fill recruitment and selection jobs?' It is concerned with being alert to the level of ability, be it sufficient or insufficient, of all those who have any part to play in the process – for example, those drafted in to supplement the activity when recruitment and selection hits a busy patch, and, more importantly, line managers who are involved in the decision-making. Just as with the general problem of acquiring human resources (see Chapter 1), there are several approaches that can be used.

Selecting recruitment and selection staff

People who are given the task of recruiting and selecting should obviously be those who have the skills. Unfortunately there are two major obstacles to achieving this. The first is identifying the abilities that are necessary to perform recruitment and selection tasks, and how these might be assessed. This is clearly within the scope of this book. What makes good recruiters and selectors is discussed below. How these abilities might be sought and measured for any given organization is the focus of Section Two of this text. The second obstacle is the influence of what might be labelled the 'organizational politics of recruitment and selection'. People are not always given recruitment and selection responsibility – they take it! They exert sufficient power to be able to make decisions regardless of their level of skill. Obvious examples are the owners and managers of small businesses, functional managers in organizations which are practically orientated towards that function, such as production managers in manufacturing companies, sales managers in distribution organizations, etc. Also line managers within these activities may well be included.

If the problem arises that those conducting recruitment and selection are lacking appropriate skills and are in a position to resist changing, then it is an 'organizational development' issue or at least one which questions the role of the personnel function.[1] Important though they may be, these issues cannot be dealt with here. In contrast, those involved in recruitment and selection who are imposed may be willing and able to change if necessary. Recognition of shortcomings in ability by those senior to them, or indeed by themselves, may lead them to either withdraw, at least in part, from recruitment or selection activities, or offer themselves for training – a pious hope but not unheard of.

Part of acquiring human resources in recruitment and selection is, therefore, the important monitoring of those involved, such as line managers, whose job is something other than recruitment and selection, in order to judge their ability to perform the task. A 'division of labour' between personnel specialists and technical specialists is often manifested in the differences between the 'personnel' interview and the 'technical' interview. This difference is discussed in Chapter 10.

In selecting recruitment and selection staff, there is a need here to make a distinction between recruitment and selection as previously defined. Recruitment is normally a specialist function, which relies heavily on previous experience. Skill level is often directly related to this experience. The ability to design a recruitment procedure, knowledge of the geographical and skill aspects of the labour market, skill in writing advertising copy, are all examples of desirable attributes of the good recruiter, plus being sensitive to the need to seek outside advice, often of a technical nature, in the recruitment of highly specialized personnel. Being involved in these activities over a period of time and across a wide range of jobs increase the competence of the recruiter. For this reason, this particular activity is normally entrusted to a personnel department, or, in the smaller organization, to the personnel specialist.

Selection, on the other hand, is not in the same position. Firstly, as has been said, it is not an activity solely carried out by a personnel department and, secondly, experience does not necessarily produce a higher level of skill.[2] Selection, like recruitment, is a broad activity. The components of that activity can be listed as follows:

1 *The perusal of application forms* If some structured procedure for pre-selection is in operation (see Chapter 9), this is a crucial stage. The selector needs to know, precisely, how to interpret the data on the application form, in line with that structure. Inevitably some pre-selection is taking place anyway; albeit unstructured and unvalidated. There are dangers of making grossly inaccurate predictions from which such things as particularly tidy or untidy writing, place of education, and leisure interests, etc.

2 *The administration and interpretation of standardized selection tests* This requires not only an understanding of what the text is measuring and why this is relevant to the particular selection case, but some appreciation of the nature of the measurement itself.

3 *Undertaking the selection interview* This raises what is, in practical terms, a central issue to the whole area of selection, 'What makes a good interviewer?' As practice or experience are in themselves not enough, which individuals within an organization should either be encouraged or discouraged from participating in this activity? The obvious answer is clearly those who do the job well. Unfortunately, we often cannot assess that until it is too late. Therefore we need to search for human characteristics which differentiate good from bad interviewers.

There are difficulties in agreeing an acceptable, observable measure of a 'good' interviewer. Research has not provided us with a great deal of evidence. At the broad level, it has been suggested that women make better interviewers than men, as they are less influenced by irrelevant information, but this is only based on a statistically significant difference between the average performance of a small group of men and a small group of women, and certainly should not cause selection to become a 'ladies only' activity.[3] Recently is has been argued that there are three components of the selection interviewer's job: representing the organization to the candidate; gathering information on candidates; and assessing candidates.[4] While on the face of it these might seem straightforward, they do embody the high level skill of being able to relate to the interviewee, an attribute which has traditionally simply been described as 'having rapport', but more recently has been described as possessing some of the delicate skills of the 'counsellor'.[5] This means, ideally, we are seeking selection interviewers who have some degree of understanding of or empathy with candidates' feelings, who are prepared to accept these by being non-evaluative, and who can exhibit a degree of genuineness or sincerity. This has the effect of narrowing down the field of potentially good interviewers.

4 *Making selection decisions*   This task is often contained in 1, 2 and 3, but not necessarily so. It is feasible to have a selection procedure, especially one which adopts the assessment centre practice, where the decision to hire or not is based on information from testing and interviewing and other sources, such as application forms and references, but is carried out as a separate activity. But, regardless of whether it is a separate activity or not, it is important for a selector to be a 'good judge'. But good judges are hard to find, because:[6]

a   much of the time people's judgements of each day are wrong.
b   much of the rest of the time people's judgements are vague and unverifiable.
c   most people avoid realizing a and b by deluding themselves about the way they judge others.

While this is a view about people in general, it is nevertheless supported by the low demonstrated validity of selection assessment procedures. It has been pointed out,[7] however, that people become better at making predictive judgements the narrower their task and, as was discussed in Chapter 3, judgements over a small range of attributes appear to have some possible validity. This is important in identifying who will make a good judge for selection. Someone who knows the job being selected for intimately might make more accurate judgements about a candidate's ability to do that job than someone who is more familiar with the organizational context in which the job exists.

Consider the case of the organization wishing to recruit a computer maintenance engineer to work with one of its computer installations. The personnel department, in seeking technical help in this selection task, might be well served by using the maintenance supervisor on that installation as an interviewer and setting him or her the task of investigating the candidate's ability to work with such an installation. This is instead of using the management services manager whose brief is to assess the candidate's suitability as a member of the management services department. This is an example of trading off breadth for accuracy. Both are desirable but sometimes a choice has to be made.

Some evidence on the attributes of good judges has been offered.[8] The better judges are those who are skilful with words, non-conforming and independent, open-minded, energetic, self-confident and optimistic. They are not dominating or gregarious. They do not submit or dominate, run or fight, they interact. They are not chronically preoccupied with their own conflicts and fears and are not people with strong emotional reactions. As this evidence is based on a laboratory study using film and pen portraits, it must be interpreted with some care in the selection situation. That does not mean it can be ignored.

In summary, therefore, the acquisition of *recruitment* staff is not particularly a problem and is usually fixed as a function of the personnel department. The resourcing issue is much more serious in relation to *selection*, because in many cases the selection process goes beyond the personnel activity. Who these selectors might be should be determined by considerations other than status.

Training recruitment and selection staff

The second method of acquiring recruitment and selections resources is, of course, through training. If those involved do not appear to be sufficiently good at it, then knowledge, skills or attitudes can be changed in order to bring about the desired behaviours of a good recruiter or selector. Because of the reasons stated above, the problem here is again with selectors rather than recruiters.

Tester training

Standardized testing in selection can range from the straightforward measurement of skill attainment, for example a speed test for a typing job, to the measurement of personality, for example measurement of temperament to cope with a dangerous or solitary job, especially one involving high technology. At the straightforward attainment end of the scale, the skills required of the tester are relatively unsophisticated and involve becoming familar with the mechanics of the measuring device, such as under what conditions the test should be taken, how the test should actually be administered and how it should be scored – the interpretation often being nothing more than whether the candidate gets above or below a predetermined pass mark. The amount of training that is required in this instance is minimal, and often a written manual will suffice, but only if the test meets the following criteria:

1 The candidate fully understands why this ability is being measured.

2 To the candidate, the content of the test clearly represents that ability.

3 The abilities being measured are clearly observable to the tester.

4   The scoring procedure is totally unambiguous.

5   The only interpretation is to relate the score to a pass mark not determined by the tester.

If the test does not meet these criteria then it is dangerous to rely on simple written guidelines as the training method. If we consider, for example, firstly a typing speed test and secondly a typing accuracy test, it is easy to see how such tests would quite easily meet these criteria. However, if it was a combined speed and accuracy test and the tester had to make some subjective assessment of the interaction of speed and accuracy, that is how much inaccuracy would be compensated for by a high level of speed, then it might be seen not to meet the criteria and might require more elaborate training.

One of the dangers of selection testing is the assumption that all tests require only this simple level of training. This can easily lead to inaccurate unethical and even illegal selection decisions. The problem is that so much selection testing concerns itself with 'hypothetical concepts'. Notions such as intelligence, interests and personality are not directly observable or easy to interpret. Testers need some grounding in the theoretical bases of these concepts and require some acquaintance with the measurement issues involved, including their statistical foundations. This is, of course, in addition to the mechanistic characteristics of test administration, which are themselves complicated by the nature of the concept being measured. Tester training, therefore, normally requires some sort of training course. In practice there is a simple relationship. The more intangible the attribute being measured the longer the training course required.

A further consideration is that psychological testing, like other areas of psychology, has a sizeable sprinkling of dubious practitioners. In order to ensure that those who use psychological tests do so to an acceptable standard, the chartered body for psychology in Great Britain, The British Psychological Society,[9] has produced a 'Certificate of Competence in Occupational Testing' scheme which has been backed by the major test publishers and the Institute of Personnel Management. These publishers will not supply tests to those who do not hold this certificate. At present the scheme applies only to ability tests but it is intended that it will include personality measures in the future.

The actual length of training programmes varies, but a rough guide would be a two-day programme for training in interest questionnaires, a further five-day programme for training in aptitude testing, and a further five days for training in personality measurements. The interest and aptitude courses initially devote some time to introduce the psychological concepts involved, the statistical techniques necessary to understand the nature of the measurement, and the administrative and scoring procedure. The aptitude courses have to concentrate considerably more on the administration procedures and scoring procedures, as these are often more varied and more complex. The personality training programme usually assumes those attending have had some experience in aptitude measurement and therefore moves quickly from statistical considerations and concentrates on the difficult task of interpreting test scores in this area of measurement. It is probably worth bearing in mind that there is some debate at present as to whether the level of skill that is attainable after a five-day programme is sufficient to allow an individual to correctly interpret aptitude test scores or whether this should be left to a trained professional psychologist. Another word of warning is that these training programmes are designed to train individuals to use standardized published tests. They are certainly not designed to enable participants to go away and design their own tests, which is a difficult and time-consuming task to do correctly.

Interviewer training
Improving the interviewing resource by training is widely practised. The training of experienced middle managers to participate in the seasonal graduate selection 'milk-round' is commonplace, as is the training of recent and not-so-recent entrants into the personnel activity. The inclusion of interviewer training in managment development programmes is another area of popular activity, and there are, of course, others.

Nevertheless, two important points must be made. Firstly, it cannot be assumed that training will actually impart all the necessary skills that a selection interviewer requires,[10] as these skills encompass counselling-type attributes which might be a function of personality more than ability. Secondly, it is much more likely that the effect of training will be to improve the reliability of selection decisions, rather than the validity,[11] that is, trained interviewers are more likely to make more consistent decisions but not necessarily better ones.

As with selection testing, interviewer training is undertaken in the form of short courses, ranging in length anything from one to ten days, but, unlike selection testing, while this training is undertaken by commercial consultancies and educational institutions, the use of internal programmes using no outside agencies is widely practised. A further dissimilarity to selection testing is the lack of accreditation of interviewer training courses. Organizations wishing to 'buy in' training expertise should examine what they might be committing themselves to very carefully.

In order to illustrate what an interviewer training course might contain, the following is offered as an example. It is a programme with which the author has had some involvement and reflects the desirable selector attributes discussed earlier in this chapter.[12] What was advocated in the design of this programme was that the skill of handling and assessing the feelings of candidates – that is, what they mean rather than what they say – is as important as the skill of gathering factual information about the candidate.

The training programme is set out below. It normally lasts for three days although shorter and longer variations have been adapted. It assumes a student:tutor ratio of 6:1. The length of each session is not fixed but is determined by the needs of the particular group being trained.

Interview training programme (adapted from Lewis, Edgerton and Parkinson)

     Sessions

	1	Group building
During	2	The criteria problem and selection decisions
the	3	Fact finding (audio recorded)
course	4	Handling feelings
	5	Undertaking the interview (audio recorded)
After		
the	6	Self-monitoring of on-the-job interviewing
course		

Session 1: Group building After a brief introduction describing desirable interviewer behaviour, the fundamental skills of listening and understanding are introduced by getting students to work in changing pairs, disclosing aspects of their own lives as material for the exercise. This highlights differences in ability in listening and understanding and, because of the mutual disclosure, creates a working group. This is essential in interviewer training, as the group itself will be required to provide a large amount of the resource material during the training programme. As a very important part of the learning of interviewing skills is the giving and receiving of feedback, a cohesive, supportive work group is absolutely essential.

Session 2: The criteria problem This focuses early in the programme on the difficulty of making selection decisions and how it is essential to have a detailed knowledge of the job being recruited for in order to have a hope of making an accurate selection. It is undertaken in the form of an exercise which causes students to make very different selection decisions on the same criteria because of their insensitivity at this stage to the ambiguity of that criteria.

Session 3: Fact finding Again using an exercise, this focuses on the skills of managing an interview by using the time correctly, and using appropriate questioning techniques and summaries in order to maximize the accuracy of the information the interviewer is collecting.

Session 4: Handling feelings   Here the student is introduced to counselling skills[13] as a way of developing a good relationship with the interviewee, which is important to the quality of the information being exchanged and also to the recruitment aspect of the interview. Two important features of this session and the previous one are, firstly, that they require a great deal of structured feedback from other course participants, which appears to be necessary for the acquisition of successful social skills such as interviewing.[14] Secondly, the exercises in these sessions do not require role-played behaviour, which appears to relate very poorly to real behaviour.[15]

Session 5: Undertaking the interview   As the title suggests, this is where the course participant is required to undertake a full, uninterrupted interview with someone from outside the course, normally the sort of person that they would be interviewing in their job, again receiving feedback.

Session 6: Self-monitoring on the job   This is not a session within the three-day duration. The trainee interviewers are made to realize that all a training programme can hope to do is to make only a small change in their actual interviewing skill at that stage, but it can provide them with criteria for monitoring their own performance. They are sent away with the task of checking this, over a large number of interviews that they have to do in reality – essentially by answering the question at the end of each interview 'How could I have done that better?' In order to aid this stage, audio tape recordings of Sessions 3 and 5 for each individual participant have been made. The participant then takes the tape, which not only contains their performance but also the feedback they received, away with them as a permanent reminder not only of their level of performance but also of their shortcomings and suggested ways of improvement.

It is naïve to assume that through the medium of a short course a 'bad' interviewer will be changed into a 'good' interviewer. It also cannot be assumed that all those entering a training programme come in with the same level of skill, or that they will respond equally to the training. Thus, an interviewer-trainer with six students, or participants, has to handle six different programmes and it is important to recognize this.

Ideally, interviewer training should be about imparting to potential selectors the desirable attributes which were discussed in the first part of this chapter. It has, however, been argued that, in practice, interviewer training is requested for one or more of the following reasons:[16]

1   To improve selection decision-making
2   To improve recruitment skills, that is attract candidates
3   To reduce interviewer anxiety

The suggestion is that 3 is easy to achieve in training, 2 is distinctly possible, but 1 is probably unlikely, for while training can equip a selector to collect better quality information and make him or her aware of how difficult it is to do something useful with it, it does very little to actually teach him or her how to use it validly. This does not mean that aiming at better decision-making is a lost cause. Indeed, it has been suggested that this is likely to be, for the future, one of the more valuable approaches in research aimed at improving the selection interview.[17] This is the subject dealt with in Chapter 11.

The method of instruction which has been the focus of the above discussion has been the training course. The traditional method of industrial training, namely sitting with, or being coached by, an experienced practitioner of the skill, is not forgotten. It is limited in tester training by the requirements of the test distributing agencies. In interviewer training it can be used with effect. It is of course cheaper and therefore attractive to the small organization. Its success rests entirely on the ability of the 'expert' or coach to be able to interview well. It therefore raises the question 'How do we know that this "expert" can interview effectively?' This method of training should only be attempted where this question can be answered satisfactorily.

Training may not provide too many answers to the problems posed by selection interviewing, but there is sufficient evidence to suggest that it is nevertheless worthwhile.

Rewarding those involved in recruitment and selection

The third method of acquiring suitable human resources is to remove any unattractive aspects which might dissuade suitable employees from taking part. The bright, ambitious, young graduate working his way up a large organization may see recruitment and selection as a bit of a backwater in times of economic recession and somewhere he should avoid being placed. He may feel that it will damage his progress to spend time gaining experience in an activity which he feels may be labelled as not of major importance in the current business climate. Also, managers, both those with line responsibility and those with functional duties, consider an involvement in the selection procedures as being a hindrance to their proper job of managing. Both these situations can and should be avoided, in order to maximize the recruitment and selection resource, by emphasizing the importance of such an activity, especially in times of recession. The cost of making bad selection decisions, especially during this sort of period, has been discussed at length in Chapter 1. What must be avoided is a downgrading of the importance of recruitment and selection, which could result in a loss of status of those working in it.

The manager who sees his involvement in the activity as not important is failing to recognize that the ability to make good selection decisions, and indeed carry out a good selection interview, is almost universally an important part of a manager's job. However some organizations fail to recognize this. For example, there is the case of the organization where recruitment is almost entirely at the bottom of the organization and the selection is carried out by those at the fourth level of management. All hiring decisions have been made at this level in the organization, but this particular activity is considered to be a very minor part of their job.

As a more general indicator of the problem, the question can be asked 'How many managers, when being appraised, have their ability to carry out selection interviews and make selection decisions accurately brought into question?' The possession of good selection skills, be it in personnel staff or in managers, should be recognized and indeed built upon by the organization.

Using outside agencies

By far the quickest way of increasing the recruitment and selection resource is to hire it in from outside as and when it is needed. This means using recruitment consultancies or agencies to handle some part of the recruitment and selection procedure. This can range from using the local Job Centre to furnish the organization with possible candidates when a vacancy occurs (or the commercial equivalent which is an agency which provides this service alongside its provision of temporary staff), through to the recruitment consultancies, who may mount a major advertising campaign on your behalf, administer a wide range of selection methods, and present you with the 'ideal' candidate, or at least a rarefied shortlist.

More specifically, external consultants can be used as a recruitment resource – 'Your brief is to present us with a good pool of applicants. We will be responsible for our own selection from there on.' Or as a purely selection resource – 'We have got this shortlist of candidates; can you please advise us as to which one we ought to appoint.' The advantage of using outside agencies is that they are convenient. An organization has instantly available to it specialist recruiters and selectors when the need for such specialists arises, and using them removes the cost of permanently employing staff who might be under-utilized much of the time.

There are disadvantages that must be considered. Like most commercial consulting and advisory activities, many are expensive in relation to the service that they actually provide, and organizations which use outside agencies because of their low frequency of recruitment may find that if their need for hiring staff suddenly increases using an agency can become considerably more expensive than developing internal recruitment and selection resources.

A second and more serious disadvantage is related to control and responsibility. In using such agencies an organization is handing over control of part of the recruitment and selection activity to an outside body which does not have the ultimate responsibility for making the hiring decisions. Even if the consultancy provides the organization with the 'ideal' candidate, the organization is left with the final responsibility of saying 'yes' or 'no'. If the recommended candidate proves to be unsatisfactory, an organization has little come-back other than to choose not to use that consultancy again, unless of course it can be demonstrated that there was blatant negligence which could be deemed as a breach of contract.

An example of this is the case of a respected recruitment agency which was given the task of recruiting a senior medical officer for a local authority. A suitable candidate was identified and subsequently hired. It was later found that his medical qualifications were bogus. In a case of this kind it is clear that the recruitment agency should carry some responsibility.

A further related problem is that the outside agency will have, by definition, only a 'second-hand' knowledge of the job being recruited for and must rely heavily on job specifications and descriptions as submitted by the client organization. This can sometimes be used as a justification for inaccurate advice offered to the client organization.

Client organizations do, however, have some protection afforded them by the Employment Agency Act 1973. This Act was initially set up to protect those seeking employment rather than those offering it, but in practice the latter group does benefit. The Act requires agencies which involve themselves in placing people in jobs to be licensed by the Department of Employment. Licensees are then governed by a Code of Conduct. This Code of Conduct is largely to prevent recruitment agencies from setting up under false pretences. It protects candidates by ensuring that their application is correctly recorded and processed, and by requiring evidence that the employer is respectable and that proper job specifications have been provided. It protects the client organization by requiring that a written quotation of the cost to the client is provided before the assignment is taken on, and that only two-thirds of the fee can be charged before any appointment is made.

One of the problems with the Act is that it covers only those agencies which offer a placement service for which they charge fees, either to a candidate or to the client organization (licensed agencies are not allowed to charge both for the same appointment), and which carry out the placement activity through the agency name. What this means in practice is that agencies which simply give selection advice, that is those which might be presented with a shortlist of candidates and asked to advise on which one the organization ought to hire, are not in fact covered by the Act, neither are those agencies which carry out the recruitment activity using the name of the client organization. Thus, if a recruitment consultancy says to a client organization 'Yes, we will place an advertisement for this particular job, but place it under your organization's name', then they are outside the Act and do not require the control of a licence.[18] This point might be worth noting when deciding which outside agencies to use.

A final word of warning. It is very easy to fall into the trap of using outside agencies as a way of delegating the recruitment and selection responsibility. The responsibility for a hiring decision cannot be delegated in this way. An outside agency is, strictly speaking, simply a recruitment or selection method.

Summary

It is wrong to assume that recruitment and selection is easy and that anyone can do it. Interviewing and selection test interpretation, for example, are complex skills. Seniority or managerial experience are not enough to justify involvement, although politically it may be difficult to prevent it.

Selectors should be carefully selected themselves, as it appears that certain personal qualities lead to better decision-making. A responsible decision for the owner of a small business to make would be to delegate the selection task to someone else if he recognizes that he lacks these qualities himself.

Training in selection interviewing skills is certainly worthwhile, and training in the skills of testing is essential.

If an organization wishes to increase its selection resources it must encourage the talent within its ranks to want to be involved. Being good at selecting should be considered a desirable managerial quality.

The quickest way to acquire recruitment and selection resources is to use outside agencies. But these can be expensive for what they provide. They rarely take responsibility for the final selection decision.

References

1 S. Tyson and A. Fell, *Evaluating the Personnel Function*, 2nd ed. (Stanley Thornes 1992).
2 N. Schmidt, 'Social and situational determinants of interview decisions: Implications for the employment interview', *Personnel Psychology*, 29 (1976), p. 79–101.
3 C. Fletcher, 'Sex and the Interview: A case for Positive Discrimination?', paper to the Annual Occupational Psychology Conference of the British Psychological Society (Warwick, January 1983).
4 R. Bayne and C. Fletcher, 'Selecting the selectors', *Personnel Management* (June 1983).
5 R. Bayne, 'Interviewing' in D. M. Davey and M. Harris (eds.), *Judging People* (McGraw-Hill 1982).

6 M. Cook, 'Perceiving others: the psychology of interpersonal perception', in Davey and Harris (eds.), *Judging People.*

7 Bayne and Fletcher, 'Selecting the selectors'.

8 H. C. Smith, *Sensitivity Training* (McGraw-Hill 1973).

9 *Certificate Statement Register, Competences in Occupational Testing* (The British Psychological Society, Leicester 1991).

10 Bayne and Fletcher, 'Selecting the selectors'.

11 R. D. Arvey and J. E. Campion, 'The employment interview: a summary and review of recent literature', *Personnel Psychology*, **35** (1982), p. 281–322.

12 C. Lewis, N. Edgerton and R. Parkinson, 'Interview training: Finding the facts and minding the feelings', *Personnel Management* (May 1976), p. 29–33.

13 L. E. Tyler, *The Work of the Counsellor*, 3rd ed. (New York: Appleton-Century-Crofts 1969).

14 M. B. Shure and G. Spivack, *Problem Solving Technique in Child Rearing* (San Francisco: Jossey-Bass 1978).

15 A. S. Bellack, 'Role-play tests for assessing social skills: are they valid', *Behaviour Therapy*, **9** (1978), p. 448–61.

16 C. Lewis, 'The value of research findings for interviewer training', paper to the Annual Occupational Psychology Conference of the British Psychological Society (Warwick, January 1983).

17 C. Lewis, 'What's new in selection', *Personnel Management* (January 1984), p. 14–16.

18 D. C. Duncan, 'The impact on psychologists of the Employment Agencies Act, 1973', *Journal of Occupational Psychology*, **50** (1977), p. 217–24.

7
Understanding the job: the development of criteria

A clear understanding of the job is the keystone of the recruitment and selection process. It provides the recruiter and selector with a more tangible target towards which the design of the procedure can be directed. It has always been one of the mysteries of this area that the simple logic of improving selection decisions by being aware of the detail of the job being selected for receives such cursory treatment in so many organizations. Individuals will gladly accept positions on selection boards without a second thought about their lack of knowledge of the job, and will then contribute forcefully to the decision-making. The fact that selectors, sometimes, have a less than adequate knowledge of the job is even more surprising since it is difficult to find a personnel management textbook that does not strongly advocate the use of some form of specification as the basis of the criteria for selection.

An accurate understanding of what a successful candidate is going to have to do makes sense in both recruitment and selection. The recruiter needs to know, for example, whether or not an engineering job is largely one of practical 'troubleshooting' or theoretical design, in order to cast the net appropriately. In selection it is even more important, as a lack of understanding will negate the whole predictive principle. It is the selector's acknowledgement of the maxim 'If you don't know where you're going, you'll end up somewhere else'. In their defence, organizations will often argue one or more of the following:

1 The drawing up of thorough specifications is administratively inconvenient, especially if they need frequent updating.

2 The final selection is being made by the immediate supervisor of the job who therefore has a very detailed understanding of it.

3 So much selection is not for specific jobs, but concerns itself with general suitability to the organization, for example graduate recruitment.

These arguments are not to be dismissed, as they present a reasonable case, but they do need answering, as follows:

1 Preparing some form of specification is time-consuming but, as was discussed in Chapter 1, the cost of the bad selection which will result

from not doing so can be so high that an organization ought to accommodate any inconvenience. Further, having gone to the trouble of preparing a specification, the resulting information is of course valuable. Firstly, it helps to monitor the impact of technological change on job content, and, secondly, it is of benefit to other personnel activities, for example training, performance appraisal, and job redesign, etc. One issue is the level of analysis that is required and this is commented on later in this chapter.

2   The immediate supervisor will have a detailed view of the job, which should be capitalized upon in selection, with his or her involvement in the writing of the formal specification. This will provide a structure that can be applied to what otherwise might be a less than objective understanding of the job. The value of using the supervisor for this task is that he or she is likely to include implicitly the question 'What sort of person would I like to work with?'; this is not to be ignored as it is a potential influence on the eventual job performance of the new hiring. The value of using a specification is that it is more likely to reduce the effect of the related, but less constructive, sentiment of 'I don't want people who can perform the job better than I could, as I may find it difficult to manage them'! If a formal written statement of desirable attributes has been made, it is harder to ignore them.

3   It is true that detailed specifications do not provide the criteria for all selection situations. Often what is needed is some formal statement of departmental or functional criteria or even organizational criteria. Dealing with different criteria levels is difficult but not impossible. However it requires discussing at some length.

Levels of criteria

The 'job' that the selector is party to filling cannot always be well-defined in terms of his own brief. There are different levels of specificity of criteria. For example, it might be that the task is to choose the candidate for a 'job' simply described as: *a* to successfully perform as a member of the company, or, more specifically, *b* to perform successfully somewhere in the computing activity of the company, or, even more specifically, *c* to train as a computer programmer to work on pension fund investments within the company.

As discussed in Chapter 3, the more the selection task involves identifiable jobs which have been concretely specified, the easier is accurate prediction of job performance. Thus, in this example, the selector will find task *a* more difficult than task *c*.

Developing organizational criteria

It is unusual for organizations to have, on file, well-developed and useful criteria to determine suitability of applicants to work within that organization. This does not mean attempts are not frequently made to develop them. It is more a question of whether they are useful or not. When it is stated, it is often in the form of a 'party line' consisting of self-evident, vague, abstract concepts such as 'Candidates selected by the company should be those who are seen as bright, able and flexible self-starters, motivated to get this job done'. A selector faced with these criteria is given little help in identifying and assessing what these qualities actually look like, and it is also difficult to envisage a situation where a selector would not be seeking these anyway. One approach to the problem is to argue that organizational criteria can be dispensed with. Anyone entering an organization is going to have some job to do when they join and it is this that should be specified in detail to help make the selection decision. This, however, ignores that there may be the firm intention that the individual moves on from this job and develops a career within the organization.

To disregard the issue of organizational criteria can, therefore, lead to mistakes being made in the assessment of aptitude. Understanding which attributes of its employees an organization considers valuable is obviously important in making judgements about a candidate's potential to develop.

How do you develop organizational criteria? To start with, it is necessary to accept the fact that there is no objective truth waiting to be unearthed by meticulous research that would specify the characteristics that pre-determine all job success within an organization. Organizational criteria are something which is perceived by each individual within that organization. But there are enormous differences between individuals' perceptions. Just what that perception is becomes important if the individual is being involved in making selection decisions. The subjective nature of those criteria will influence the selection decision if the individual has got no information to suggest, firstly, that his or her perception is wrong, or, secondly, that it is not shared by other people. Organizational criteria can be identified by selectors, be they personnel specialists or managers, by displaying and sharing their perceptions in order to achieve some degree of consensus. This does not produce an organizational success specification, usable on all occasions, but it reduces the degree of subjectivity which is inevitably applied in answering the question 'What sort of people get on in this company?'

A procedure to share perceptions in this context is as follows:

Step 1 Assemble together a group of individuals who will be involved in selection decisions resting on organizational criteria. This can include personnel staff and/or managers. Ideally the numbers should be between six and twelve; a number less than six is insufficient to explore the range of individual differences in perception; if the number exceeds twelve, it makes the procedure very difficult to administer.

Step 2   Each member of the group is asked to write down on a piece of paper, which no-one else will see, the names of approximately five successful company hirings whom they are personally acquainted with, success being defined not necessarily by organizational advancement but by the statement 'If the company had its time over again it would have no hesitation in recruiting these people'. This list can contain those who have not advanced particularly far, but who are content to stay where they are, and perform extremely well. Similarly, the group members are asked to write down a list of about five names of those whom they would consider to be unsuccessful hirings. This list should not necessarily contain only those who have made little advancement or who have been dismissed, but can contain those who have advanced faster than the organization can cope with. Again, a useful instruction would be 'If the company had its time over again it would not recruit these people'.

Step 3   Group members are then asked to consider their two lists as two groups of people, perhaps even to picture them as standing in opposite corners of a room, and to think of any adjectives that could be used to differentiate the two groups.

Step 4   Write up on a blackboard, or flip-chart, a column headed 'Successful' and a column headed 'Unsuccessful'. Collect from each member up to three differentiating adjectives. It is likely that the adjectives will apply to one of the groups with the assumption that the negative form of it applies to the other group. For example, one member, on reflection, may have identified his successful group as being generally 'considerate' and therefore the unsuccessful group are seen as 'inconsiderate'. This cannot be permitted in the translation of the adjectives on to the blackboard, otherwise it would preserve the abstract quality of the adjectives which renders it of little practical value in identifying criteria. Each member must, therefore, identify the adjective as it describes eithers the successful or the unsuccessful group, but may not use the opposite negative (sometimes positive) form of the adjective. Ideally, a brief behaviourial phrase should be provided. This more clearly defines what that individual sees as being the difference between his or her two groups. In Example 7.1 the word 'inconsiderate' cannot be used to give the opposite meaning to 'considerate'. The individual must substitute a phrase to describe the unsuccessful group which might be either *a* 'they tend to give their subordinates a tough time', or *b* 'they are only interested in themselves and their own jobs'. This provides a much clearer indication of the individual's perception of what is meant by 'considerate'. It has a different meaning if opposed to *a* than if opposed to *b*, a difference which is usable in selection because it is partly being expressed behaviourly, that is if a candidate presents evidence that he or she has managed people in the past by giving them a tough time, and that that is his or her preferred style, then the suitability of that candidate may be called in question.

The adjectives and their opposing phrases are entered under the appropriate column headings. The numbers of adjectives and opposites being offered by group members will often decline as this collection procedure progresses. Some members will claim that those already offered are identical to their own.

Example 7.1 *Organizational criteria*

Successful hirings	as different from	*Unsuccessful hirings*
Considerate		'Give subordinates a tough time'
Flexible		'Only want to work in their specialism'
'Have got to know the right people'		Politically naïve
Self-motivated		'Always need targets from their bosses'
'Consider the job to be more than nine to five working'		Undedicated
'Prepared to wait for promotion opportunities'		Highly ambitious
Confident		'Easily persuaded to alter decisions'
Socially skilled		'Have little influence on the behaviour of subordinates'
etc.		etc.

Step 5 What has been derived with some degree of empiricism are two lists of adjectives and phrases describing behaviour. Those under the heading of 'Successful' are an indication of what the organization should be seeking when selecting. Those under the heading 'Unsuccessful' are an indication of what it wishes to avoid, as produced by this group of selectors. Obviously there will be differences of opinion and some adjectives will be challenged. Group consensus should be used to decide whether an adjective should be retained in the list or not.

The group finally decides how the elicited characteristics to be sought and those to be avoided can best be assessed within the selection procedure.

The value of this exercise to identify organizational criteria is twofold. Firstly, it actually provides data which is useful to the selector in his or her decision-making and, secondly, by going through the process, each selector becomes aware of how idiosyncratic his or her views are of what are valid criteria. What is often enlightening is not what the list contains but what is absent. It has, for example, been my experience, in carrying out this exercise on numerous occasions with managers involved in graduate recruitment, that adjectives such as 'bright' and 'intelligent' do not appear, even though, to many, these would be considered the most obvious criteria. Here the exercise is indicating that bright and intelligent hirings, especially as measured by academic attainments, turn out to be unsuccessful as often as successful. If this is the case, then the graduate selector must be careful not to place too much weight on apparent measures or intellect.

The procedure outlined above, while being a little crude, is fairly quick to undertake, and easy to administer. A more sophisticated approach, which involves structured interviews with individual managers or others in the organization, and requires the services of a suitably trained psychologist, involves the use of the Repertory Grid.[1] This technique, originally designed as a method of assessing an individual's personality structure, is now being used to assess how managers structure their own 'perceptual maps' of the organization, or specific roles within it. It is not widely used but its popularity is growing. As it is time-consuming and usually involves employing an outside consultant, it is costly. However, this technique is a useful aid in developing organizational criteria and individual job criteria for some managerial posts.

Briefly the technique can be applied in a number of ways. These are derived from the original design of the grid.[2]

To elicit these 'perceptual maps', the interviewee (usually a manager) is asked to name ten to fifteen 'people'. These might be key people listed by name, for example other managers to graduate recruits, etc.; key roles such as a first-line supervisor, a technologist, a departmental manager, etc.; or people of specific type – these may include someone who performs well, someone who appears happy in their work, or someone who finds their job irksome, etc.

These names are called 'elements' and comprise the horizontal side of a grid or matrix. The interviewee will then be asked to consider three of these elements, saying in which way any two are similar but different from the third. How the interviewee describes the similarity and difference is considered to indicate one of the ways in which he construes his environment.

Let us assume that the elements are ten named managers. The interviewee is also a manager from the same organization. He is presented with three of the names from his list (for example, name B, name D, and name E) and asked to consider them as indicated above. His rsponse is 'B and E are similar because they are both easy to approach on work matters, but D gets annoyed if anyone goes to him'. This would indicate that one of the ways in which the interviewee views managers in the organization is as whether they are approachable or unapproachable. Thus 'approachable – unapproachable' would be labelled as a construct and entered as the first line on the vertical dimension of the grid.

Each of the remaining seven names are then rated by the interviewee as either closest to 'approachable' or 'unapproachable' (using ticks and crosses on the grid).

Another three names are then compared which will produce another construct. This becomes the second item on the vertical dimension. The 'ticks' and 'crosses' are entered under each name for this construct.

The comparing of names in threes is continued, producing more and more constructs until all the combinations of names are exhausted, or the constructs start to repeat themselves – the result is a grid where the vertical is a list of constructs which represent the individual way that the interviewee classifies his work environment. These are each related to the managers or roles which are listed on the horizontal.

Organizational criteria can be identified by examining the grids of a number of managers, or others, in the organization. This does present a problem. By definition, the constructs are personal to each interviewee, which prevents cross-comparison. But the patterns of 'crosses' and 'ticks' can be statistically analysed to determine the pattern of inter-relationship of constructs – it is this analysis and subsequent interpretation which usually requires specialist professional skills.

The development of function or department criteria

This is the half-way house between the vagueness of organizational criteria and the precision of job specific criteria, where recruiters and selectors often find themselves. They frequently have to make decisions as to the suitability of candidates to work within a stated department or function. Engineers are clearly more likely to be offered jobs in engineering, computer scientists in computing, and arts graduates in the non-technical administrative departments. Ways of developing criteria in these cases are as follows:

- To carry out a similar exercise to that discussed in relation to organizational criteria. The difficulties, however, are firstly, getting sufficiently large selector teams for the exercise from one department, and, secondly, as there is the distinct possibility that the group will know each other extremely well, the exercise can become politically very sensitive.

- The use of sophisticated statistical methods. Within the confines of the structure of a department it is possible to identify a criterion of success, namely the position or grade that someone has achieved in that department. It is therefore possible, although again politically sometimes difficult, to identify those who have made senior grades, and examine to see if they differ in any way from those who have not advanced to that level, even though they have been with the organization for approximately the same length of time. A statistical technique which can be used is called 'Discriminant Function Analysis', which is described in the discussion on pre-selection in Chapter 9. The reason why such a technique can work at a departmental level but is not advocated at an organizational level is that in the latter case the use of progress as a measure of job success is more difficult to justify, as the assumption will have to be made, for example, that the arts graduate in the marketing department and the engineering graduate in the production department have equal opportunity for advancement.

- If an organization has carefully specified each individual job in some detail, it is possible within the department or function to examine all the specifications and look for the elements which appear to be common to most. For example, within a marketing department it is likely that most jobs will specify that their incumbents possess a high degree of communication skill, both written and verbal. This would then become immediately identifiable as one of the departmental selection criteria.

The development of individual job criteria

Making no apologies for repetition, what cannot be over-emphasized is the importance and value of a thorough, structured understanding of the job being recruited for, in order to improve the accuracy of selection. How is this thorough understanding arrived at?

The traditional approach

This is undertaken by drafting a detailed specification, firstly by concentrating on the job itself and, secondly, from this, the necessary aspects of the person who might fill the job. It is a process of job analysis which results in a job description; this becomes a job specification, enabling a person specification to be drawn up.

The logic of this is simple, but it often becomes confused in practice. This is largely because the terminology is not universally agreed upon. For example, some organizations will interchange the terms 'description' and 'specification', or others may use 'job specification' as a general heading which incorporates the 'person specification' and so on. However, the labelling of stages is less important than adherence to the logic, and here lies another problem. It is possible to follow the procedure, but miss the point. 'Identify the job; understand its important features; and recognize the relevant human aspects of its successful performance' can easily become 'Take a job title; list its components; and itemize the characteristics of an acceptable candidate'. If this is the case, important elements of the analysis have been omitted. These are the ones that give the selector the 'feel' for the job. Questions that need to be answered, such as 'How is the job more than just a collection of tasks?', 'What do incumbents actually like and dislike about it?', 'Are we willing and able to develop the shortcomings in otherwise good candidates?' remain unresolved.

In essence, this is a warning against the over-mechanistic approach to job analysis. A highly structured and detailed form on which job/person specifications are drafted can produce this effect. Filling in the form accurately becomes the overriding objective rather than conveying a real understanding of the job. Also, the problem can arise if those writing the specifications are different people from those who will be using them to make selection decisions, especially if they have been drawn up as part of a blanket job-analysis programme within a department or the whole organization. When people fail to recognize the specifications of their own jobs, or selectors ignore those prepared for them as being genuinely unhelpful, these are signs that the analyses may be missing the less tangible but important aspects of the job.

This is certainly not to argue against the systmatic preparation of job and person specifications – quite the opposite, in fact – but to point out that the real need is for the selector, be it a personnel specialist, line manager or the owner of a small business, to have an accurate understanding of the job in question. A well prepared job/person specification is an effective way of providing this.

What a job analysis should contain has been discussed by many authors in the personnel management field. The job analysis checklist in Example 7.2 is an amalgam of some of these suggestions, but with special attention being paid to the issues raised above.[3]

It is referred to as a checklist because it not only provides the headings to allow thorough job and person specifications to be drawn up, but it also acts as an *aide-memoire* to the selector to what he must find out

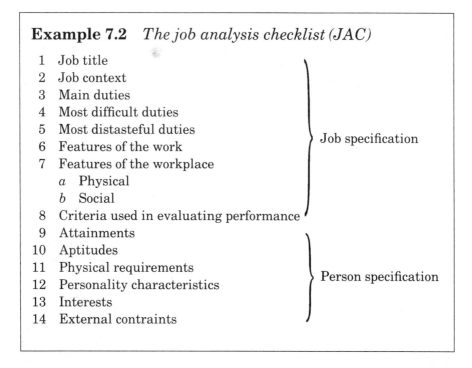

Example 7.2   *The job analysis checklist (JAC)*

1   Job title
2   Job context
3   Main duties
4   Most difficult duties
5   Most distasteful duties
6   Features of the work   } Job specification
7   Features of the workplace
    a   Physical
    b   Social
8   Criteria used in evaluating performance
9   Attainments
10 Aptitudes
11 Physical requirements
12 Personality characteristics   } Person specification
13 Interests
14 External contraints

about the job if he is going to make valid selection decisions. At the very least, it brings home what he does not know. Points 1 to 8 constitute the job specification, points 9 to 14 the person specification. However, they should be taken as one list. All are important to the selector throughout the selection process.

While a checklist of this sort is convenient, it must not be seen as simple to use. For this reason, in order to understand more fully how it operates, familiarity with the first section of this book, especially Chapter 4 which discusses important psychological concepts, is strongly recommended.

1   *Job title*   The formal job title, together with its departmental and geographical location, should be recorded in full. A vague job title might result in a job specificaiton being used in the recruitment and selection for jobs which are significantly but not obviously different. One aspect of title that can cause problems is whether a trainee is a different job from a fully trained person. Does a trainee warrant a job specification in his or her own right? The answer depends on whether the incumbent will automatically move into a trained position, or will have to go through some form of selection at the end of training. If the former is the case, then it is desirable

not to have a separate job specification and to cope with the issue of training under step 10, *Aptitudes*.

2   *Job context*   It is important to consider why the job is done. How does this job relate to other jobs that are connected with it? (This should also include vertical relationships, that is, who does the incumbent report to, and who reports to the incumbent.) How is the job linked to the overall objectives of the department or entire organization? It has been suggested that this part of the specification is often defective because personnel specialists do not have sufficient information available to them.[4] This means that whoever is going to use the specification for selection may need to talk to management services or manpower planning departments if the organization is large.

3   *Main duties*   This entails a list of the main duties and responsibilities of the job which can be derived through discussion with present incumbents and their supervisors, together with actual observation of the work being done. Often a useful source of this information is annual appraisal reports, as these may contain an updated set of duties agreed between boss and subordinate. This should not just include frequent duties, as many infrequent activities are essential to the job. Special care should be taken in listing the duties to avoid certain verbs which are ambiguous in behavioural terms, for example, 'liaise', 'co-ordinate', and 'take responsibility for'. Further, if the job being specified is one of a supervisory nature, the use of these descriptive words can result in the duties of a subordinate being listed instead of those of the supervisor. One of the problems with a straightforward list of duties is that they are not equal in terms of their difficulty, important or frequency. As candidates will have different strengths and weaknesses in their likely performance of the duties, then it is often useful to apply some kind of weighting to suggest which duties should command the most attention during recruitment and selection. For the moment, this can be considered to be a separate activity and is described later in this chapter.

4   *Most difficult duties*   It is most useful for recruitment and selection purposes to identify the most difficult of the duties from the list.[5] This can be achieved by asking job incumbents what they find the most difficult parts of their job, and asking immediate supervisors what they observe to be the most difficult duties. This highlights the part of the job that is particularly vulnerable to failure. The sort of question that can be asked of those who are responsible for supervising the job can be 'In cases of unsatisfactory performance, what seems to be the particular problem area?'. The qualities

necessary to perform difficult duties are those that demand special attention during recruitment and selection.

5   *Most distasteful duties*   In the same way as difficulties highlight areas of unsatisfactory performance, distaste can highlight areas of dissatisfaction for the job incumbent. However, this should be directed not at the main duties but at the job as a whole. Again, job incumbents can be asked directly 'What is the most irksome aspect of your job?', and supervisors can be asked 'What seems to cause people to quit or ask for a transfer?'. The value of such a question is that it often throws up features of the job which are not readily apparent but need to be borne in mind during recruitment and selection, for example, pay, poor public transport, unacceptable managerial style, or low public regard for the job. These should feature in the recruitment and selection process and care be taken that they are not 'brushed under the carpet'.

6   *Features of the work*   This refers to aspects of the work rather than the workplace, which are likely to affect the job-holder, such as the work being heavy, unvaried or dangerous, etc. Here information can be collected by direct observation, as well as by interviewing those who are familiar with the work. All it is asking is that the unexpected aspects be noted. There is little point in recording, for example, that a typist will be required to work at a job which is not heavy or dangerous.

7   *Features of the workplace*   This is a consideration of the immediate environment in which the job exists. It is divided into:
   a   Physical – is the workplace dark, dusty, damp, or does it have extremes of temperature, etc.?
   b   Social – is the work solitary, or does it involve a team? Does the team tend to be co-operative or competitive? What sort of style of supervision exists?
Aspects of the environment that need to be highlighted are those which might be considered extreme or unexpected. Again, there is little point in noting that a typist will work in an office that has a temperature within the legal limits. It certainly would be worthwhile noting if it were not within those limits.

There may seem to be some degree of conceptual overlap between points 6 and 7. It is worth, therefore, emphasizing that there is an important practical difference. Features of the work itself suggest to the selector those aspects of a candidate's abilities or work record that need investigation. Features of the workplace suggest that it is the candidate's attitudes and willingness to adapt that is more the focus. For example, certain jobs in the operation of off-shore oil-drilling platforms are dangerous, heavy, damp, and involve extremes of temperature. In selecting for these posts, the first two features would be part of the job itself, and it would be important that applicants had successfully coped with these job features in the past. The second two would be part of the workplace. The selector would be seeking assurances from the applicant that he is willing to accept such physical conditions.

8 *Criteria used in evaluating performance* This is really to answer the question 'What sort of people get promoted out of the job to the next level?'. This indicates the criteria which are actually used in evaluating job performance. It can be a salutary lesson because it is often different from what might be expected. If it is different, then some attention should be paid to this at the time of selection. An example might be a shorthand typist who is chosen for promotion to the grade of secretary largely because of his or her level of interpersonal skill as demonstrated during their time as a shorthand typist. But this might not have been considered important when the individual was selected. It is a more fruitful approach to understanding what the organization, in reality, values in the job than asking 'What will be regarded as normal performance?'

9 *Attainment* What is actually meant by attainment and how it differs from the next heading of *Aptitudes* are very important in specifying the sort of individual that is needed to fill the job. For this reason it is necessary to consult Chapter 4. Suffice to say here that attainment is a statement about what the organization is aiming to 'buy in' by hiring an individual for this job. What skills and knowledge will he or she bring, and what educational and occupational experience should recruiters and selectors be seeking as indicative of these? In practice, it is usually the major element of the person specification.

10 *Aptitudes* In summary, this refers to the abilities that successful candidates must possess in order to be developed in a certain direction. This is especially important when the successful candidate is definitely, or even likely, to be involved in some training, and also if the job is the first stage of a career within the organization.

11 *Physical requirements* Clearly this is where a note is made concerning requirements of the job such as height, freedom from disability in limb movement, or colour blindness, etc. Restrictions of age and sex can also be considered here, bearing in mind the issues discussed in Chapter 5.

12 *Personality characteristics* Enduring traits – for example, being socially outgoing, having a democratic approach, or being self-reliant, etc. – which are required for successful performance of the

job should be noted here. As personality is an important but frequently misused concept, look again at Chapter 4 before completing this task.

13   *Interests*   What kinds of outside work interests are important for people to successfully perform the job? Investigating how people spend their spare time is a common feature of selection, especially a selection interview, but, as we have discussed before, the occupational relevance of some of these activities is limited. However, some aspects of interest can be relevant. For example, it might be important to the job to know if candidates spend their spare time as active members of an organized group or team, maybe having some leadership role in it, or if they have interests that highlight administrative skill. If it is necessary to the selection decision that these areas are investigated, then this should be noted here.

14   *External constraints*   This really means external constraints that the successful candidate must be free from. Constraints might, for example, prevent the job incumbent from being away from home, working anti-social and irregular hours, or having holidays that do not coincide with the school holidays. Yet, in practice these could be part of the job. Clearly if one of these is a feature of the job, it must be noted and communicated to applicants before a hiring is made. It is these aspects, which, like the distasteful ones, are sometimes overlooked by recruiters and selectors, although occasionally they are conveniently ignored. It is a short-sighted approach, of course, as it could quickly appear that you have hired an employee who is unable to perform the job properly.

These fourteen headings, therefore, constitute a job analysis checklist (JAC). The information on the points listed can be derived from observing the job being performed, interviewing those already employed in it and their immediate supervisors, and becoming acquainted with any relevant data that might be held by departments such as management services. This is not to overlook the benefit of the recruiter or selector simply spending some time on 'thinking the job through' under these headings.

In examining the JAC, it was suggested that it is sometimes worthwhile trying to identify the relative significance of the various duties to the ultimate performance of the job. This is useful in discriminating between candidates whose differing talents fit different duties. Each duty has a degree of importance to the overall job, offers some degree of difficulty, and is performed more or less frequently. Trying to assess the significance of any duty to recruitment and selection is complicated by the fact that these three qualities interact. There is clearly a difference between a difficult duty that is important and a difficult duty that is unimportant. Further, those which occur infrequently provide the person doing the job with little opportunity to improve performance of that duty. Thus, for an important but difficult task which is infrequently performed, special attention must be paid so that only candidates with the ability to cope are hired.

Based on this logic, a schema, the 'Main Duties Weighting' (MDW) can be used to evaluate each duty. This is shown in Figure 8. It is operated by tracing each duty, in turn, through the schema. This provides a simple weighting on a 1 to 3 scale. The high scoring duties are those which should command the special attention of the recruiter and selector. The recruiter should aim at attracting candidates who, at least, will be able to perform duties weighted '3'. The selector must ensure that these duties will be successfully performed by those hired. The low scoring duties are less critical at the time of selection.

For example, in the selection of an office-block security guard two of the listed duties might be:

1   Check identity passes of people entering the building.

2   Eject threatening, intoxicated or abusive individuals from the premises.

The first of these may be adjusted to be important, not difficult, and frequent. Using the MDW it would score '1'. The second may again be seen as important, but this time difficult and infrequent. It would score '3'. The first is less critical at the time of selection because someone hired, provided their eyesight and reading ability were adequate, could soon learn this part of the job. The second is of greater concern to the selector. If it is not investigated at that time, it might not become evident that it is a shortcoming of the hiring until he or she has to perform it, and fails – with serious consequences.

The JAC (with MDW) is designed to provide for anyone undertaking recruitment or selection, be they personnel specialists or line managers in a large organization, or the owners of small businesses, a structure to aid their understanding of the job that is to be filled. As stated earlier in this chapter, to use a job analysis form that has been completed by someone else may not facilitate this understanding. It is the very process of considering the job against the fourteen headings which can produce an insight into the important aspects of job performance. Those involved, especially in selection decision-making should, therefore, complete the form. Selection, despite any statistical or computerized methods that might be used, still relies, in the end, on judgemental prediction of job performance (see Chapter 3). Judgement without understanding is not recommended.

More recent approaches
The use of the Repertory Grid has been mentioned as a tool for deriving organizational criteria. It can also be used in identifying individual job

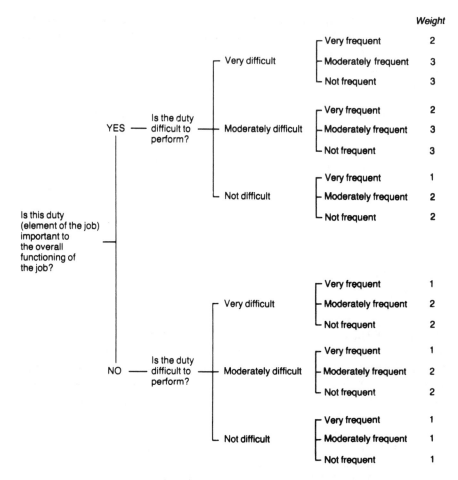

Figure 8   *Schema for Main Duties Weighting (MDW)*

criteria. It is the job incumbents and their immediate supervisors who need to be given the structured interview in this case.

This approach has great potential in the job analysis field and has high face validity to those introduced to it. The drawback is that it is often inaccessible to the small employer as it requires outside, specialist expertise. Ironically, it is a technique that could suffer if it became widely practised, as it relies, to a large extent, on the naïveté of the interviewee as to what is going on. Also, widespread use would almost inevitably produce a dilution of the expertise required to use it.

Other approaches aim at empirically determining the aspects of the job that provide the key to predicting successful performance.

One such technique has been used by the Procter & Gamble Company, Cincinatti, Ohio, in the selection of production workers in plants producing soaps, detergents, toiletries and food, and paper products.[6] It was an attempt to describe key features of the job in a sufficiently behavioural way so that selectors could identify and examine past behaviours of candidates which were similar to desired future behaviours.

To accomplish this, questionnaires were administered to those already in posts, and supervisors. These were supplemented by interviews. The responses were factor analysed (this is a multivariate statistical technique – see Chapter 3) and the elements of the job appears to 'cluster' together into the following five factors:

1   Stamina and agility
2   Willingness to work hard
3   Working with others
4   Learning to work
5   Initiative

Each factor was defined by a number of descriptive statements. For example, learning the work was defined as:

> 'Ability to learn quickly and effectively. Being able to assimilate a good deal of factual information in a relatively short period of time. Understanding work directions. Being able to keep different instructions clear in mind. Ability to quickly become self-sufficient.'

These, therefore, became five behaviourally defined 'what counts' factors. Candidates passed through a series of interviews which were firmly structured around these factors. A guide was produced for interviewers on how to gather, categorize, and document descriptive evidence under each of these. Selection was made using predetermined decision rules related to the factors – for example, a weakness in one cannot be compensated by a strength in another.

In evaluating this approach, it was found that it enabled employment interviewers and line managers to assess, with a high degree of reliability, the capabilities of applicants, male or female, black or white. The validity of the selection decision was, it was hoped, enhanced by the behavioural link between a candidate's history and the key features of successful job performance.

Another attempt at using a behaviourally based method has been to design an 'accomplishment record inventory'.[7] Dimensions of the job were elicited by asking a large sample of job-holders to identify what they would describe as major accomplishments in the job. Here, the much tried and tested method of 'critical incident analysis'[8] was used. The job-holders were asked to describe how they actually behaved in incidents which they felt were indicative of accomplishing good job performance. The accomplishment data were evaluated by those who were senior and well-respected amongst the professional group which was the focus of the study (legal attorneys). The information was converted into a rating scale which was related to actual behaviour (this is technically referred to as a 'Behaviourally Anchored Rating Scale'). This scale, when used to rate the suitability of experienced candidates, was found to be a reasonably good selection predictor. It must be pointed out that the evaluation of this method offers no evidence as to its suitability for occupations other than that of attorney, or whether it can be used on candidates with no training or experience in the type of work involved.

Both the behavioural approaches described above have the disadvantage of only being possible in a large organization where there are many similar jobs (for example, those of production workers), or in small organizations that employ staff who have to possess nationally recognized qualifications and experience (for example, solicitors, chartered accountants, etc.). But they do have an important message for all those involved in recruitment and selection: that there are definite benefits in focusing job analysis on what the job actually involves the holder in doing in an observable sense.

These benefits are that decision-making can be improved because selectors have a degree of understanding which enables them to concentrate on 'samples' rather than just 'signs' of predictive behaviour in the candidate.[9]

Finally, the issue that needs to be mentioned is the application of the concept of 'competences' (see Chapter 4) in the development of job performance criteria.[10] These are used to explain the practical capabilities that an effective job incumbent should possess. Whilst, on the face of it, this is an inherently sensible approach, it has been hindered by a failure to define or assess adequately the nature of a competence. The confusion would seem to lie in deciding whether it is an aptitude, a skill, a combination of the two, or indeed is related to traits of personality.[11]

As there is currently substantial British Government support and investment in competence-based performance standards, there should be hope that efforts will be made to remove the confusion.[12]

Summary

To have any hope of achieving accuracy, those involved in recruitment and selection must have a clear understanding of the nature of the job which is the focus of the recruitment and selection.

One problem may be that it is unspecified; the task is simply to bring people into the organization. In this case, organizational criteria need to be developed. This should be done by those making the selection decisions. Selecting individuals to work in a stated department or function can equally mean that jobs are unspecified. The solution may be to approach the problem in the same way, but here there is often more hard evidence available to answer the question 'What sort of people get on in this department?'.

In recruiting or selecting people for a specified post, methods of job analysis are used. Traditionally, these have utilized job and person specifications. These have stood the test of time and are applicable to almost any specific job selection situation, regardless of size or nature of the organization. However, they are sometimes 'mechanistically' drawn up and fail to convey sufficient understanding to the user. it is important that the person making selection decisions goes through the analysis process himself – even at a cursory level. A job analysis checklist (JAC) is offered for this purpose.

The trend in current developments in job analysis is to concentrate on the key behavioural aspects of the job, in order to enhance the selectors' understanding in the decision-making process.

Care in the development of recruitment and selection criteria is as important to the owner of the small business as it is to the personnel specialist in the large organization.

References

1 V. Stewart and A. Stewart, *Business Applications of Repertory Grids* (McGraw-Hill 1978).

2 G. A. Kelly, *The Psychology of Personnel Constructs*, vols I and II (New York: Norton 1955).

3 P. Ribeaux and S. E. Poppleton, *Psychology and Work – An Introduction* (Macmillan 1978).

  G. Thomason, *A Textbook of Personnel Management*, 4th ed. (IPM 1981).

  P. R. Plumbley, *Recruitment and Selection* (IPM 1976).

  J. Munro Fraser, *Employment Interviewing*, 5th ed. (Macdonald and Evans 1978).

  A. West, 'Recruitment and Selection', in *A Textbook of Techniques and Strategies in Personnel Management*, D. Guest and T. Kenny (eds.) (IPM 1983).

  A. Rodger, *The Seven Point Plan* (NIP 1952).

4 Thomason, *A Textbook of Personnel Management*.

5 Munro Fraser, *Employment Interviewing*, 5th ed.

6 D. A. Grove, 'A behavioural consistency approach to decision-making in employment selection', *Personnel Psychology*, **34** (1981), p. 55–64.

7 L. M. Hough, M. A. Keynes and M. D. Dunnette, 'An evaluation of three "alternative" selection procedures', *Personnel Psychology*, **36** (1983), p. 261–76.

8 J. C. Flanagan, 'The critical incident technique', *Psychological Bulletin*, **51** (1954) p. 327–58.

9 P. F. Wernimont and J. P. Campbell, 'Signs, samples and criteria', *Journal of Applied Psychology*, **52** (1968), p. 372–6.

10 R. E. Boyatzis, *The Competent Manager* (Wiley 1982).

11 W. Hirsh and S. Bevan, *What Makes a Manager* (Institute of Manpower Studies 1988).

12 *Management Challenge for the 1990s* (Training Agency and Deloilte Haskins and Sells 1989).

8
The recruitment phase

Armed with the knowledge of what to look for in suitable candidates, the process of recruitment can be commenced. Its object is to provide enough interested people to enable selection to be undertaken. It is important to see the recruitment and selection phases as distinct. Failure to do this may mean that the implications of whether manpower is abundant or scarce might be overlooked, resulting in the inefficient use of recruitment or selection resources (see Chapter 2). In discussing aspects of recruitment in this chapter, it will be assumed that it is for a specified job unless otherwise stated.

Generating the applicant pool

As recruitment tends to be more of a centralized function than selection, the recruiter needs to possess the skills to recruit for posts across the whole organization or unit. Unfortunately, there are two influences on recruitment over which the recruiter may have little control. Firstly, he or she may be asked to generate applicants for a job that has a title which will mean very little to those outside the organization. Titles such as 'Project Co-ordinator' or 'Technical Liaison Officer' require further explanation to convey any meaning, and this may be difficult within the confines of a job advertisement. Secondly, those in recruitment are saddled with the public image of the organization, which may be a help or a hindrance, either nationally or locally. The national image stems from its products or services, the local image depends on the local experience of employment in that organization. Attempts are made to attack the problem of public image, but these are rarely instigated by personnel departments, although obviously they welcome them. One example is the practice of presenting 'prestige' advertisements using television and the press. These do not make reference to any particular product – for example, Philips claim to be 'simply years ahead', and British Petroleum is 'Britain at its best'. A second example is the sponsorship of leisure activities and socially acceptable campaigns – for example, Cornhill Insurance's involvement with test cricket, and the Ford Motor Company's £20,000 contribution towards the 1983 Conservation Awards.

Another area that might be largely outside the control of a centralized recruitment activity is what might be described as 'informal recruiting'. This is where new hirings are a result of informal contact or direct approach from managers or any member of the workforce. This sector of recruitment must not be underestimated. In 1982, 34 per cent of employees were in fact recruited through relatives or friends.[1]

There are also the hirings that result from casual enquiries. As the initiative has come from the applicant and not the recruiting organization, it suggests a level of enthusiasm which the organization would be wise to respond to, by having a procedure that can immediately cope with such an enquiry.

Recruitment sections of personnel departments do, however, have a high degree of control over the more formal methods of recruitment and these need to be examined.

Methods of recruitment

One way of classifying these methods is to distinguish between those that the organization undertakes itself, by trying to make direct contact with potential applicants, and those that involve getting others to make the contact. Whatever type is chosen it is important that the recruiter has carefully considered and understood the job analysis and weighted the main duties within the job specification. The results of this might be reflected in the content of any recruitment method of the first type, and in the brief given to the outside agency when using the second type.

The direct contact methods are internal and 'on-site' advertising and media advertising.

Internal and 'on-site' advertising

This involves informing employees of vacancies through the use of noticeboards and internal broadsheets and, where suitable, displaying a notice outside the premises in order to attract the attention of passers-by. These methods have the advantage of being cheap and often considered politically prudent. Clearly, they can help prevent redundancies. They also enable the internal workforce to act as recruiters who often make good-quality recommendations. (Special attention is necessary here to prevent illegal indirect discrimination – see Chapter 5.) They have the obvious disadvantage of only reaching a limited population of potential applicants. An interesting phenomenon with regard to internal advertising is that some organizations find themselves, through agreement with the trade unions, obliged to advertise vacancies externally, for example the teaching profession, whereas others, also through agreement with the trade unions, must advertise internally in the first instance, and can only advertise externally if a suitable candidate is not forthcoming.

If candidates have been recruited internally it should not be forgotten that they are different from those attracted from outside. Rejected internal candidates remain in the organization. For this reason, selection should be seen as thorough and fair. Internal candidates should be assessed to the maximum that the selection procedure will allow. In practical terms, this may mean adhering to a rule that 'all internal candidates should be interviewed'.

Media advertising

In practice, this refers to the national, local, or technical press. Using television for recruitment is rare because of the prohibitive costs of a sustained campaign. A recruiting organization would be paying a large part of the fee to reach an audience in which they have no interest. Local commercial radio is being used to some extent, but here there is a problem of no visual impact. Press advertising is, of course, familiar territory for most commercial and industrial organizations, both in relation to product advertising and recruitment advertising. However, there is often a marked difference in how these two are handled. Product advertising will come through a marketing department, will often attract a much higher budget, will be carefully planned in advance, and those responsible for it will have a clear idea of what they are trying to get it to produce. Recruitment advertising, which might emanate from a personnel department containing largely amateur marketing skills, is designed and inserted often at short notice, with the vague objective to produce suitable applicants. The result is that job advertisements are less cost-effective than they might be. It has been argued that the basic aim of this kind of advertising should be to recruit at economical costs. To achieve this, four 'rules' have been suggested.[2]

1   Advertising must set out to communicate with an appropriate audience. This entails an accurate appraisal of the labour requirements in relation to the media coverage to ensure that the right audience is addressed.

2   The advertisement should produce an adequate number of replies. For one appointment the attraction of 100 replies is surely a mark of failure to communicate properly. An accurate assessment of the market is an essential element of a company's recruitment advertising. An adequate and select number of replies is sought for shortlist purposes.

3   The advertisement must also minimize the number of wasted replies and the consequent unfruitful time spent on the administration of unsuitable applications. Wasted replies mean extra work. Minimization results not only in a more satisfactory solution for the selection officer, but also reduces the number of disappointed applicants who merit an early rejection.

4   It is highly desirable that advertising should seek to build a

continuing image of the company as an employer, for long-term purposes. Not opportunities should be missed to promote an organization as a progressive and desirable employer. To this end, every advertisement can project a long-term recruitment image. If well done, advertisements will inevitably attract some applicants to make contact without waiting for specific job advertisements to appear. These guidelines clearly indicate that it is the role of the recruiter in using press advertising to aim for an optimum number of suitable replies. One advertisement that was placed in 1983, seeking management trainers and offering a salary in excess of £20,000, asked only for applicants to be of graduate level with some managerial or consulting experience. It appeared in the national press and gave very little additional information. Needless to say, it produced a huge response, as a large number of people, attracted by the salary, would meet the rather vague criteria.

The fundamental recruitment skills therefore, in relation to press advertising, are twofold. They lie, firstly, in preparing the content of the advertisement and, secondly, in knowing where the advertisement should be placed.

There are two small dangers here that recruiters need to be alerted to. Advertising copy should be aimed at attracting the desired type of applicant, not at pleasing the recruiter's boss; and the content of that copy should not be altered because of the particular newspaper or journal in which it is to appear.

Writing job advertisements

In short, the task is to communicate with the reader by attracting his or her attention by presenting the necessary information, using the smallest amount of space, thus cutting costs. However, powers of attraction and cost need to be balanced to give a satisfactory outcome. This depends on the visual style of the advertisement. It has been suggested that there are a number of factors that are helpful in gaining attention.[3] They are:

1 The position on the page
2 The use of white space – can be used to convey the image of an 'up-market' company
3 The design of border and graphics – can have a dramatic effect in gaining attention
4 The headline

It is the task of the skilled designer to combine these to achieve the optimum cost/attention balance. It must, of course, be pointed out at this stage that press advertisements are normally placed via advertising agencies who can offer useful advice on layout and visual presentation.

While they will charge for services such as artwork, advice will often be provided free, as they receive payment from the publication.

The content is also important. The following are the items that should be considered for inclusion in an advertisement.

- *The name of the employing organization*   This should be written so that it is easily seen. It is a mistake, however, to allow the company name to take up most of the advertisement's space, in the belief that the name alone will attract applicants. This is no longer the case. If the nature of the organization is not generally known, it is worth adding a brief (one sentence) description of what it does, for example 'Machine-tool manufacturer in the automotive industry'. Some advertisement are written without revealing the name of the employing organization and carry anonymity to the point of including a box number instead of an address. While there might be all sorts of reasons why the company might wish to operate in this way, it must be remembered that it does arouse suspicion amongst potential applicants.

- *Duties of the job*   This is where the recruiter needs to consult the main duties weighting (MDW), discussed in the previous chapter. Selective duties which are clearly weighted as '3' are those which should be outlined at this stage. They are the core of the job, and applicants can decide if they are attracted by them or not. This is particularly important for non-routine, technical, administrative or managerial posts. To add more special emphasis, the most difficult duties (as described under point 4 on the JAC) should be highlighted.

- *Unattractive features*   This is where recruiters often lose their nerve and are tempted to disguise some of the unpleasant aspects of the job. This can be an unwise step to take. What is entered in the advertisement is based on the JAC point 5, distasteful aspects, with possible additional information from points 6, 7 and 13 – features of the work itself, the workplace, and external constraints. This information is necessary to facilitate self-selection on the part of potential applicants. It does not mean it should be written in order to shock or to say 'Come and join us if you dare', but to gently convey the reality of the job.

  A good example of this appeared in an advertiment for the post of Head of Personnel in a national Sunday newspaper. Within the copy appeared the following sentence 'On a personal level, a stable and understanding domestic situation will be necessary to meet the commitment and the significant UK travel required to take advantage of the good promotional prospects'. This indicates to potential applicants that the job is likely to impinge considerably on their home life, which could become disrupted. The organization expects them to tolerate this. The implication is that, not only would they be unsympathetic if a domestic situation were used as a reason for poor performance, but it would be seen as a justification for not promoting the job-holder. An individual, who might otherwise be a highly suitable applicant, may decide that the post is not what he or she wants and therefore not waste everybody's time by applying. To disguise this potentially unacceptable aspect of the job from the candidate until after he or she had been selected, would, of course, have been disastrous not only for that candidate but for the organization.

- *Rewards* Jobs can offer both tangible rewards – for example, salary and perks – and intangible rewards – such as status and prestige. Potential applicants are, of course, interested in both, but it is only feasible to mention tangible rewards in a job advertisement. Statements concerning intangible rewards lack credibility. One way round this is to express status in the form of the job's reporting responsibility – for example 'the person occupying this position will report directly to the Director of Marketing'. To describe a job as high-status may well arouse suspicion. What potential applicants want to know is what the salary is, or the salary range, and what, if any, are the other 'fringe benefits' – for example, company cars, cheap mortgages or free private medical insurance. These constitute just about the only objective criteria that an applicant can use, at this stage, to evaluate the job. It might be, of course, that this peculiarly British practice of offering fringe benefits is actually a tangible statement of status.

  While this is the information that applicants want, it does not necessarily follow that employers are prepared to give it. A case is often made for salaries not to be disclosed, as it might be a dissatisfying influence on existing staff. This might be the case, but it is difficult to know how this can be kept a secret for long. Not revealing salary level in an advertisement reduces the number of applicants, which might be a good thing. However, as disclosed in Chapter 2, arbitrary actions to reduce applicants may reduce the administrative load but can also have the effect of ruling out highly desirable candidates. A frequently attempted compromise between revealing or not revealing salary levels is to recommend that only salary earners at a certain level should apply. This is, however, fairly transparent, as most applicants would take it to mean that the salary on offer is the figure quoted plus a negotiated amount of make the job-change worthwhile. Thus, on balance, it is generally better to identify the salary and the fringe benefits.

- *How to apply* This information, which should normally come at the end of the advertisement, must not be treated as self-evident to the applicant. What that applicant has to do to pursue an interest in the job must be made very clear. Should he or she send a full *curriculum vitae* to the organization? If so, precisely to whom and by when? Does it require that the applicant should make contact by either writing or phoning in order to be sent an application form? It would be a pity to destroy the work that has gone into the carefully designed advertisement by ending it with ambiguous and difficult contact instructions that cause good candidates to either be lost or lose interest.

Placing an advertisement

As one of the aims of press advertising is to communicate with an appropriate audience, the skill of placing is to know which newspaper or journal is likely to reach that audience. The data that are important to the recruiter are those which are derived from the analysis of newspaper readership in terms of social classification. A widely used system is given in Table 1.[4]

Table 1

Social status		*Head of household's occupation*
A	Upper middle class	High managerial; administrative; professional
B	Middle class	Intermediate managerial; administrative; professional
C1	Lower middle class	Supervisory or clerical; junior managerial; administrative; professional
C2	Skilled working class	Skilled manual worker
D	Working class	Simply skilled and unskilled manual worker
E	Lowest level of subsistence	State pensioner or widows; casual or lowest grade workers

Therefore each newspaper can be assessed in terms of what percentage of each social class it attracts. For example, in the mid-1970s it was reported that *The Times* was read by 21 per cent of social class A and 10 per cent of social class B, but the *Daily Express* was read by 26 per cent of class A and 27 per cent of class B. However, the *Sunday Times* attracted a higher percentage from both social classes. What the recruiter has to do is to match these data against the charges that different newspapers make for advertising space. One source of information to the recruiter is the National Readership Survey which is produced annually by the newspaper industry. This gives information about readership and social class by occupational title. The major source of information, however, concerning the costs and readership of newspapers, journals, and magazines is *British Rate and Data* (usually referred to as BRAD).

The above relates largely to the national press, but of course the use of local or technical press is sometimes appropriate. The local press is considerably cheaper, for, in paying the high charges of national newspaper advertising, like those of television, you are paying for the privilege of reaching many people whom you are not interested in. Also people who are seeking local employment will tend to turn to the local newspapers. The exceptions are those seeking technological, managerial or senior administrative posts, who will tend to look in the national press. Indeed, some national papers have almost a monopoly for some occupations – for example, senior secretarial appointments in *The Times*.

The technical press – for example, trade journals and the publications of professional bodies – has the advantage of hitting the desired population most accurately, and is relatively inexpensive, but it tends to be published infrequently and require advertising copy well in advance of publication date. Another niggling aspect is that sometimes there is more than one appropriate journal, and the readership of one is different from that of the other.

The final issue in placing advertisements is that of timing. It is sometimes foolhardy to instruct an agency to place an advertisement 'as soon as possible'. Many newspapers, both national and local, have days of the week when they specialize in certain types of occupations, thus attracting specific readers on that day. It is important that the recruiter is aware of this and instructs accordingly.

Direct contact with educational and training institutions
If an organization is seeking to employ local school-leavers or recruit university graduates, then it can pay handsome dividends to go direct to the source. This enables the organization to 'take its pick'. This point is often missed in times of unemployment because of the plentiful supply from such institutions, but, as mentioned in Chapter 2, the high cost of 'milk-round recruitment is, even now, justified on the grounds that if an organization does not actively participate it will not get its fair share of the top 5 or 10 per cent of graduates being sought by competing organizations. In the acquisition of university graduates it must be remembered that whilst the 'milk-round' has a function of selecting out inappropriate applicants, it is largely a recruitment activity. A bad graduate recruitment campaign can seriously affect the numbers of applicants in subsequent years.[5]

It is now necessary to move on and consider methods of recruitment that are, so to speak, contracted out.

Managerial and executive recruitment agencies

The use of outside agencies to produce a pool of applicants is a convenient way of buying in recruitment resources and this was discussed at some length in Chapter 6. A crude division is between those which tend to recruit managerial and executive staff, and those which focus on non-managerial staff.

This method of recruitment is costly and is most justifiable when the organization is seeking to hire someone for a unique position and therefore has little experience or machinery to deal with it itself. Thus the main benefit is that a particular recruitment expertise can be acquired as and when needed. Also, with the agency acting as an intermediary, the organization wishing to recruit can remain anonymous. Known suitable applicants, especially those for very senior posts, can be approached directly. Agencies which deal in highly specialized and senior jobs, and which acquired, during the 1970s, the label of 'head hunters' (because they give the impression that they are setting out to track down the one person to meet your needs) sometimes operate by possessing a detailed but finite list of talented individuals. The danger with this kind of organization is that they may not search beyond their list and, even after you may have employed their recommended individual, he or she will still remain on their list to be hunted again.[6]

Non-managerial recruitment agencies

Firstly, there are the commercial employment agencies, which are often better known as the source of temporary staff, especially clerical and secretarial. They are plentiful and relatively inexpensive. They also make it very easy for employers to acquire staff through them. Unfortunately, they have a reputation for not producing staff of dependable quality, and strong opinions have been expressed, for example: 'At the other extreme there are those who believe (and share at least this belief with the most militant of trade unionists) that agencies are a menace to the business world, encouraging staff turnover and pushing up expected salary to a 'buyers' market to ensure a larger fee and thereby adding to the problem of inflation.[7]

Secondly, there are government-sponsored agencies, with the most obvious example being Job Centres. A characteristic of these (and the same can be said of Professional and Executive Recruitment) is that they contain on their registers very few people who are in employment and seeking to change. Thus, recruiting through such agencies means that the organization will be dealing with largely unemployed applicants. The advantages of Job Centres are that they can operate very quickly as part of a national network, and they do not have to enter a business relationship with the recruiting organization.

Evaluation of recruitment methods

How effective recruitment methods are can be judged by the number of suitable applicants they provide, or, in the long-term, how successful the eventual hiring is. At this stage it is worth considering just the first point, the second will be dealt with in Chapter 12. Assessing the effectiveness of recruitment is one of the few aspects of the whole area of recruitment and selection that brings with it a feeling of confidence in the results of that assessment. The actual number of firm applicants that any method produces can be assessed against the cost, and this calculation has the benefit of dealing with fairly concrete figures. While it might take a certain amount of trial and error, in, for example, trying out different newspapers or agencies, it is nevertheless quite possible to predict and determine a budget for different recruitment categories. For example, the cost of one recruitment method might be made up of the advertising agency fee, the costs of newspaper space and staff time to process the replies and draw up a shortlist, other variable costs such as stationery and telephone calls, plus part of a company's fixed costs. Most of these are easy to quantify.

It is, of course, possible to undertake a more sophisticated analysis,[8] and assess the qualitative performance of a recruitment method rather than its quantitative one, that is, which method produces the best candidate. But the problem of deciding what 'best' looks like can make this exercise unrewarding.

Attracting the scarce applicant

The important aspects of this problem have been aired in Chapter 2. One of the features of economic recession is that it produces an abundance of applicants. Because this can cause such a problem to selectors, the whole of Chapter 9 has been devoted to the subject. The trouble is, however, that there is a danger of assuming that there is no such thing as scarce applicants. It is, of course, not true, and examples have already been given. How should the recruiter cope with the problem? The glib answer is he or she must simply 'try harder'. But areas of scarcity must be recognized. In practice, this means that advertising must be quickly and carefully monitored. A period of two to three days following a national press advertisement is normally enough to gauge its success and, at that time, decisions can start to be made about whether to try elsewhere.

The main source of the scarce applicant needs to be actively and directly 'attacked'. To do this it is important that the recruiter is sensitive to the nature of the labour market. Does he define it in very local or in broader terms?

A company situated in the suburbs might experience a shortage of applicants for the job of 'storeman', having advertised in the local newspaper, not realizing that people seeking these posts may be prepared to travel across the whole city for the best deal they can get.

To attract these people, the company will have to use city-wide advertising, offering the city rates of pay. Another example would be the organization that wishes to recruit petroleum engineers, but these are only produced by one university department in the UK. It will have to make its presence known to the staff and students there, taking very great care to preserve a good image.

One method of attracting the scarce applicant is by adjusting the financial rewards of the job. The danger of this is that an organization's salary structure can become distorted in order to keep an ineffective recruitment procedure intact.

Very little reference has been made, so far, to recruitment literature. In the case of over-subscribed jobs it has the advantage of presenting potential applicants with more details that might encourage them to select themselves out. For scarce applicants, how literature is presented might influence their decision for or against an organization. The care that appears to have been put into its literature can suggest the concern that the organization has for wanting to make responsible selection decisions.

A final comment. Selection methods can have a bearing on recruitment. Unfair or unprofessional methods can turn good applicants away. If they are scarce applicants, it is to be regretted.

Summary

Selection cannot happen without there being a pool of applicants. The recruitment phase is the generation of this. The image of an organization provides the baseline for attracting people, but it is a phenomenon which is usually outside the control of the recruiter. Control comes from the utilization of different methods of recruitment. Some involve direct contact with the labour market, such as 'on-site' or press advertising, or going to the source of recruits, for example, schools or colleges. Others use intermediaries such as recruitment agencies. The essence of this control is the evaluation of different methods. This is quite easy to achieve in quantifiable terms, but more difficult when the issue is quality.

The economic climate for the foreseeable future suggests that recruitment is declining in importance in comparison with selection. What must not be overlooked is that a scarcity of good candidates still exists for some jobs and in some places.

References

1 *General Household Survey* 1982, Office of Population Censuses and Surveys (HMSO 1984).
2 K. G. Fordham, 'Job Advertising', in *Recruitment Handbook*, 3rd ed., B. Ungerson (ed.) (Gower Press 1983).
3 A. West, 'Recruitment and Selection', in *A Textbook of Techniques and Strategies in Personnel Management*, D. Guest and T. Kenny (eds.) (IPM 1983).
4 Fordham, 'Job Advertising', in Ungerson, *Recruitment Handbook*.
5 C. Lewis, 'Pre-Selection: Its Reliability and Validity', paper to the British Psychological Society – Annual Occupational Psychology Conference (York 1980).
6 B. Prentice, 'Head Men and How to Hunt Them', *Personnel Management*, vol. 7, no. 1 (January 1975).
7 J. G. Knollys, 'Clerical Staff', in Ungerson, *Recruitment Handbook*.
8 R. Braithwaite and J. Pollock, 'Analysing Responses to Recruitment Advertising', *Personnel Management*, vol. 6, no. 12 (December 1974).

9
Pre-selection

The previous chapter highlighted the need for generating a pool of applicants so that selection can take place. If this is successful, it can, however, be a mixed blessing. The organization might be faced with the prospect of processing a very large number of candidates. In order to meet this problem, a procedure is something necessary to reduce the number of applicants.[1] This procedure is often referred to as 'pre-selection', a term which is clearly a misnomer. In many cases, it is the practice of 'selecting out' the majority of applicants.

Why pre-selection?

As economic conditions and technological developments are likely to mean that more and more people will be chasing fewer and fewer jobs across the whole employment spectrum, the existence of an unmanageably large pool of applicants will become a much more common phenomenon. A particularly good example of this is in the area of graduate recruitment. The large British multinationals have attracted far more applicants than there have been vacancies in almost every year since the mid-1960s. In the late 1970s and early 1980s, however, the mismatch became even more acute, a picture that is likely to be repeated in the early 1990s. Table 2 indicates the dramatic jump in number of applicants for one large employer, comparing 1979, 1981 and 1983.

Table 2 *Graduate recruitment and selection numbers for a large British company, 1979, 1981, 1983*

	1979	1981	1983
Number of applicants	3,601	5,953	8,197
Number interviewed	1,786	2,770	1,980
Number offered employment	202	236	205

The problem is simply how does an organization cope with these numbers of applicants, especially when it is seeking to take on only a small percentage of them?

Traditionally, the answer has been to use procedures which remove the necessity of interviewing all who apply. Of course, the penalties of rejecting candidates without interview are as old as selection itself. It is an obvious way of making selection more manageable and thus reducing costs. But how it is done deserves attention.

What is less traditional is to approach the task systematically – to seriously question why some candidates are rejected while others are not – at this early stage of the selection process. The concern that rigour should replace arbitrariness in this stage of decision-making has given rise to the current interest in pre-selection.

Dealing with increasing numbers of applicants by just rejecting even more through time-honoured methods is becoming unacceptable for the following reasons:

1 Realization that good candidates may be overlooked, and this could prove to be a very costly mistake (see Chapter 2).

2 Taking to heart the spirit of the legislation of the mid-1970s which removed an employer's total freedom to reject at will (see Chapter 5).

3 Concern that continued high unemployment means more dissatisfied job applicants, so the fairness of selection will be under closer scrutiny.[2]

How to 'do' pre-selection

Pre-selection usually takes place between the receipt of the application form and the construction of an interviewing programme. Clearly, this is the most cost-effective time, as it eliminates the expense of bringing candidates physically into the employer's premises or sending interviewers out to those candidates. It may involve simply the use of a normal application form, or a specially designed questionnaire that supplements or replaces it. As this is homing in on biographical information it is frequently referred to as collecting 'biodata'.[3]

The information on the application form, therefore, becomes the essential data for pre-selection decisions. How this information is handled depends on how seriously the employer is considering the hypothetical costs of bad selection. If it is simply a case of reducing the number of applicants regardless, then the only information that needs to be noted is the applicant's name and address, so that he or she can be written to and informed of the decision. However, totally random decisions of this kind are, hopefully, almost unheard of. What is much more likely to be the case is that the personnel department or various functional managers in the organization will make decisions based on small amounts of information taken in an inconsistent manner from the application forms. The individual making this decision might be simply responding to a question such as 'Which of these candidates should we not bother to interview?' Information on such items as qualifications held, interests pursued, previous jobs, or just the general neatness of presentation of the form, will be assessed differently by different individuals. Differences in values and prejudices will be unchecked.

While this type of pre-selection might be taken seriously by all concerned in order to avoid random decisions, the result may be precisely that. A pre-selection method, therefore, must deal with this by attempting to standardize the treatment of the information presented on candidates' application forms. This standardization does raise issues and these are now considered.

Criteria

As has been discussed previously, those involved in recuitment and selection are forever seeking methods that predict job performance. Pre-selection is no exception. It is not uncommon to find managers in organizations who claim that certain pieces of information about applicants can immediately classify them as successful or unsuccessful, for example someone might claim that a graduate with less than a lower-second-class honours degree can never become a successful administrator. Or, alternatively, another might claim that graduates with first-class honours degrees also never become good administrators in that particular organization. Either of these might be true, but they should not be acted upon unless they are thoroughly verified. Verification might mean more than simply producing evidence that certain sorts of graduates actually do better in the organization that others, because that in itself might disguise the existence of a self-fulfilling prophecy, that is these managers might be in a sufficiently powerful position to determine the destiny of graduate entrants so that their view is justified.

If these pieces of information are shown to be predictive and the organization is happy for this to continue, then clearly these can be used as the basis of decision-making at the pre-selection stage, albeit a rather piecemeal approach. Developing a job performance criteria that enable selection decisions to be made is, as stated many times in this book, a hazardous business. This has meant that other criteria, more objectively assessable, have been used. Thus, pre-selection criteria can be classified as follows.

Job performance   Where studies have been carried out that indicate successful pre-selection, they have been largely conducted with men in middle-class professions as the focus. They have utilized measures of performance such as supervisor's ratings or sales performance.[4] Clearly it is difficult to use actual job performance criteria when the selection decisions are based on organizational criteria.

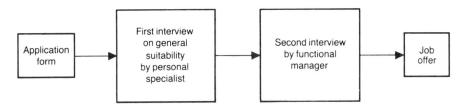

Figure 9 *Example of a selection procedure*

Employee turnover This has the advantage that it can be exactly identified. Those selected have either stayed or left. One disadvantage is that the length of tenure which the organization considers acceptable in its employees is normally subjectively indicated. Another is it makes no allowance for unsatisfactory performance amongst those who stay. Pre-selection has, for some time, been shown to be quite effective at predicting turnover, although this often refers to times of low unemployment.[5] A characteristic of studies using this criterion is that they have concentrated on women employed in clerical or unskilled manual jobs.[6]

Selection progress Attempting to predict whether a candidate will, at the end of the selection process, be offered a job or not provides an objective criterion measure. A sample of applicants will clearly contain those who eventually received offers of employment and those who were rejected.

To use this criterion has the distinct disadvantage that it assumes the existing selection process, as a whole, to be adequate. If a company is using invalid methods in selecting employees, then this fact will remain hidden in any validation of the pre-selection part of the procedure. It offers the advantage, however, of including in any evaluation the data from rejected candidates. The two other types of criteria are related to the behaviour of successful applicants after they have been employed.

One justification for using 'selection progress' as a pre-selection criterion is that the aim may be to reduce the selection task without damaging its validity, rather than attempting to enhance the validity of the selection procedure.

Method

In designing a pre-selection procedure, what is being sought is a method of interpreting application form information so that it can be used to predict future performance on an acceptable criterion. It is necessary, therefore, to develop some empirical basis for this interpretation, regardless of what type of criterion is being used. An example, using selection progress as the criterion, is as follows. It relates to a selection procedure shown in Figure 9.

The steps to take are:

1   Examine the application form currently being used. Check what information candidates are being asked to provide. Look at a small sample of completed application forms in order to gain some idea of how applicants actually respond to the form.

2   Design a classification format for the application form. This means ascribing numerical values to the information contained on the form. Different parts of an application form will present varying degrees of difficulty in trying to achieve this. It is easy to put a numerical value on the number of school examinations passed; it is slightly more difficult to put a value on distance to travel to work. But it can be assessed by checking the distance to the applicant's place of residence as shown by the addresses given on the application form. Even more difficult, but not impossible, is to put some numerical value on an area such as interests. This can be done by considering both variety and depth of interest. This stage in the process is time-consuming but pays handsome dividends in the end.

3   Extract from personnal files the application forms of as large a sample of candidates as possible who had applied for the same position in a fixed time period, for example one year. Sort the application forms into categories which reflect how the candidates actually fared: those who were rejected without interview; those who were rejected after their first interview; those who were rejected after their second interview; and those who actually received job offers. The sorted pile in which any candidate appears represents his or her performance against the selection success criterion. In order to focus on the difference between good and bad performance on this criterion, it is necessary to eliminate the middle piles in the sorting.

4   Using the application form classification format, score those in the group representing the candidates rejected without interview, and score those representing the candidates who had been offered jobs, or at least made it to second interview.

5   Examine the differences in the application form information as presented by these two groups. The quantified classification enables the observer to gain some idea of the magnitude of the difference. There are, of course, varying levels of analytical sophistication that can be applied to this stage in the process. The quickest and simplest way of determining differences between the 'unselected' and 'selected' groups is simply by inspection, especially if carried out by a group of individuals, for example personnel and functional managers, who achieve some sort of consensus in their observation and interpretation of the data. More complex analysis of the information can be achieved by the use of statistical methods. The use of percentages to identify differences in the type and frequency of information offered by the two groups of candidates,[7] or the simple

correlation of application form data with the criterion measure[8] can be used. A more rigorous method is 'Discriminant Function Analysis',[9] the details of which cannot be described here, other than to say that it is a method whereby each part of the application form is classed as a variable and each variable is considered in terms of how powerful it is at predicting whether an individual is more likely to belong to the 'unselected' group or to the 'selected' group. The variables, or aspects of the application form, that emerge as the most powerful are those that reveal aspects of the candidate which dictate whether they are likely to receive job offers or not.

6 Translate the emergent discriminating characteristics of the application form information into instructions which can be used in a consistent manner by all those having to carry out the pre-selection. This can be done by issuing recommendations (or instructions) that certain parts of the application form be evaluated as providing sound information about candidates, while other parts should be ignored. More helpful, however, is to produce a 'scoring plan' so that those assessing a candidate's form can quantify the information on a single, simple scale. The nature of the 'plan' can be derived from the statistical analysis.

7 Validate the procedure. It is not uncommon to come up with application form information which quite dramatically discriminates between the 'successful' and 'unsuccessful' job applicants. There is, however, a danger of being lulled into a false sense of security. A discriminating feature of the application form might only be temporary, even though it is quite dramatic. For this reason it is necessary to repeat the exercise using a similar group of applicants from another time period, for example repeat the exercise on the applicants from the following twelve-month period. This applies equally if you are using just the judgement of managers and others, or using sophisticated statistical methods. It is the nature of the information which continues to discriminate between those who will do well in the selection procedure and those who will do badly which should form the basis of a more permanent pre-selection procedure.

A further example, this time using job performance as the criterion, is as follows:

The steps to take are:

1 Elicit from the managers and supervisors of employees, of the type being pre-selected (for example, graduate trainees), what they consider to be the characteristic behaviours of 'successful' performance as compared with 'unsuccessful' performance for these hirings. (The methods used can be those for identifying

organizational criteria. These may include the use of Repertory Grid techniques – see Chapter 7.)

2   Design a questionnaire, the responses to which can be scored to provide information on how a candidate is likely to behave in relation to the elicited aspects of step 1 which differentiate 'successful' from 'unsuccessful' performance. This can contain questions, for example, about how he or she would react to certain instructions or has reacted in the past.

3   Draw up a series of rating scales which also relates to the elicited aspects that differentiate 'successful' from 'unsuccessful' performance. The managers and supervisors are asked to assess the present job incumbents on these scales.

4   Take from the personnel department's files the application forms of those rated on these scales.

5   Administer the questionnaire to the present job incumbents. How individuals answer is quantified and compared with the manager and supervisor ratings. (Correlation methods can be used here.)

6   If a high relationship is found, then it would indicate that the questionnaire has an acceptable degree of validity. If there is not a high relationship, then it must raise serious about the design of the questionnaire. Close examination of the questionnaire items in relation to each of the rating scales can indicate where the design might be improved.

7   An acceptable questionnaire can then be used to supplement or replace the existing application form. An applicant's score will then form the basis of the pre-selection decision.

Using employee turnover as a criterion in pre-selection can be undertaken with a combination of the two examples above. Hirings can be separated, retrospectively, into 'long stayers' and 'short stayers'. Some form of discriminant analysis can be applied to their application forms, and a suitable scoring system produced to be useful in pre-selection.

The products of pre-selection

The actual information that an application form will provide to predict selection success, job performance success, or employee turnover will clearly differ from organization to organization, from job to job, and even from time to time. In order to illustrate, however, the type of information that can be gleaned from carrying out an investigation, it is worth considering one such study.[10] This concerns an investigation into the pre-selection of graduates for administration posts in a large British company. The criterion used was that of selection progress. The aspects of the application form which were related to subsequent selection success were as follows:

1 *Extra-curricula activities*   Those who indicated on their application form a wide, yet differing, range of interests, or a small number of interests pursued at considerable depth, for example holding a position of office, such as chairman or secretary, in a particular organization, were more likely to make further progress through the selection procedure than those who showed few, or unvaried lists of interests.

2 *School records*   Those who indicated at least two GCE 'A' level subjects, with two grades of 'A', or a grade 'A' and a 'B' were much more likely to be offered a post than those with lower grades. The possession of three or more 'A' level passes had no effect, regardless of grade. It also made no difference if individuals had made two attempts at passing these examinations. Those with less than two grade 'B's were far less likely to receive a job offer.

3 *Record between leaving school and making current application, including university performance*   Applicants who had stated that they had achieved or expected to achieve at least an upper-second-class honours degree were more likely to receive a job offer. However, equally strong positive predictors were the winning of a significant prize while at University, or holding a significant post of responsibility, such as being President of the Students' Union. Also equally powerful was having been in full-time employment for at least nine months, or being highly proficient in a major foreign language, other than their first language or the language of their degree. Factors which were stong negative predictors of receiving job offers were if the applicants had obtained or expected to obtain a third-class honours degree or less, or if they had missed a year of their course or re-taken examinations.

4 *Career expectations in relationship to career to date*   In this study the applicant was asked to present information on this topic in the form of a narrative. All that was provided for this was a blank side of the application form. This obviously presented severe classification problems, but nevertheless still produced predictors of job selection success. These were the length, style and content of the narrative as written. Length was a positive predictor when all the available space was completed. It was a negative predictor when less than half the available space was used, or where the candidate attached a great deal more information by using an additional sheet. Style was a positive predictor when the narrative was adjudged to be clear, simple, well-connected and easy to read. A confused, difficult-to-read piece had a negative effect. The content was positive when the

candidate offered new information in addition to that which had been presented elsewhere on the application form. It had a negative effect if he or she simply paraphrased the details of his or her past career which had been indicated already on the form.

The above example of an actual pre-selection study was operated by scoring the actual application forms, ascribing high weights to the positive predictors and low weights to the negative predictors, aggregating the scores, and operating a cut-off point below which the applicant would not be considered for interview. Thus the low scorers were eliminated without ever having a face-to-face contact with the organization.

Does pre-selection work?

Essentially this is asking if it is reliable and valid. The issue of reliability has two aspects. Firstly, is there a high degree of stability in the information that candidates offer as biographical data (biodata) on application forms? The evidence produced some time ago suggests strongly that there is.[11] Secondly, are application form data reliably assessed by those making pre-selection decisions? In the study of graduates cited above, twenty-five managers were asked to undertake the pre-selection rating using three-point scales. As indicated, this included such matters as clarity of narrative style, and width versus depth of interests. The ratings were found to be highly reliable. (The median correlation between these assessors was $r = 0.92$.)

Thus a carefully-designed pre-selection procedure seems to have at least high reliability on its side.

As has been discussed before, the existence of reliability does not, by any means, guarantee validity. However, many of the studies which have used job performance criteria present evidence of acceptable levels of concurrent validity. Indeed, it has been argued that there are few, if any, selection methods to better the use of biographical data.[12]

Evidence of predictive validity is harder to find. This is a pity, as it would indicate whether the empirically derived weightings and scoring plans, applied to application forms, hold good over a number of years. With reference again to the study of graduates above, the pre-selection scoring scale was validated against the selection progress by taking samples of applicants going through some eight years after it was first used. Correlations were found to be within the range $r = 0.25$ to $r = 0.35$.

Although these are quite high validity coefficients by selection standards, it still means that what is causing selection interviewers to make decisions about candidates is largely information other than that which appears on the application form as interpreted by the pre-selection procedure. (The pre-selection score is explaining only about 10 per cent of variance in selection outcomes.)

Compared with other selection methods, it is probably fair to say that pre-selection does work. But why? An attempt has been made to explain the validity of biographical data[13] by accepting that there is no single reason why items that appear to predict should do so. It is a combination of the following:

1   Biographical data items are successful which share elements of the behaviour being predicted. (This is the same phenomenon which gives value to behaviourally-based job analysis methods – see Chapter 7.)

2   Human development involves a series of stages. Success at the tasks of any stage predicts success at those of later stage. For example, academic success at secondary school is predictive.

3   An opportunity structure is in operation. Father's occupation can be indicative of educational and occupational opportunities.

4   Stability is a result of financial responsibility and family commitments. The evidence of these predicts continuing stability.

Thus there is no simple theoretical explanation. But the concept of validity does not require it.

Additional points on pre-selection should be noted. Crudely operated, it may damage recruitment. If an organization is perceived by potential candidates to be using a near-random procedure, this may act as a serious deterrent to those considering applying, affecting the 'good' applicants more than the 'bad'.

A pre-selection method may also be insensitive to supply and demand differences within one category of job title. For example, graduate recruits will embrace scarce types of applicants as well as those in plentiful supply. An employer might be desperate to attract scarce computer scientists or electrical engineers, in which case he must amend or even remove the pre-selection stage for this type of applicant.

It is clear from Table 2 that some sort of pre-selection procedure is inevitable, but it produces, at best, relatively unsophisticated results. The compromise should be to use it for removing the bottom strata of unsuitable applicants; aiming at identifying for rejection the worst 20 to 25 per cent, perhaps. This might still leave a costly interviewing load, but to cut back even more could prove to be a false economy.

Finally, it is worth considering the issue from the applicant's view-point. Pre-selection based on application form data is unpopular. University appointment boards, for example, have often expressed their regret that large employers of graduates are having to operate such a system. It is an aspect of selection over which an applicant has little control or feedback. Interviews are interactive processes which can be manipulated.

If they are failed, the candidate can often identify why. Failing at the pre-selection stage may bring about a feeling of helplessness, having learned nothing about how to do it better next time.

Pre-selection practices exist and their use will increase in a climate of high unemployment. The greater the care that goes into designing the pre-selection method the more it can move away from randomness.

Summary

A serious contemporary problem in selection is how to handle the over-supply of job applicants. Resource problems often prevent all of those who apply for jobs being interviewed. Selection decisions have to be made using the biographical data presented on completed application forms. This is referred to as 'pre-selection'.

If an employer is seeking to fill a large number of similar jobs for which there are many applicants, pre-selection can be approached systematically, using statistical techniques, and producing highly reliable and reasonably valid results.

In choosing a pre-selection method there is a problem of what criterion measure should be used. Should it be job performance, employee turnover, or selection progress? There are advantages to each.

Carefully planned pre-selection seems worthwhile. Unplanned or random approaches can produce illegal selection procedures or incur long-term costs.

In general, systematic pre-selection techniques are only feasible for the large employer.

References

1 J. Wingrove, R. Glendining and P. Herriot, 'Graduate pre-selection: A research role', *Journal of Occupational Psychology*, **57** (1984).
2 C. Lewis, 'What's New in Selection', *Personnel Management* (January 1984), p. 14–16.
3 R. J. Drakeley, 'Biographical Data' in P. Herriot (ed.) *Assessment and Selection in Organisations* (Wiley 1989).
4 P. Herriot, *Down From the Ivory Tower* (Wiley 1984).
5 E. A. Fleishman and I. Berniger, 'One Way to Reduce Office Turnover', *Personnel*, **37** (1960), p. 63–9.
  A. J. Schuh, 'The Predictability of Employee Tenure – A Review of the Literature', *Personnel Psychology*, **20** (1967), p. 133–52.
6 Herriot, *Down From the Ivory Tower*.
7 J. B. Miner, *Personnel Psychology* (Macmillan 1969).
8 Schuh, 'The Predictability of Employee Tenure'.
9 G. Stainer, 'Improving "Milk-Round" Methods', *Personnel & Training* (February 1969).

10 C. Lewis, 'Pre-selection: Its Reliability and Validity', paper to the British Psychological Society Annual Occupational Psychology Conference (York 1980).

11 W. A. Owens, J. R. Glennon and L. E. Allbright, *A Catalog of Life History Items* (Greensboro N.C.: Richardson Foundation 1966).

12 R. R. Reilly and G. T. Chao, 'Validity and fairness of some alternative employee selection procedures', *Personnel Psychology*, **35** (1982), p. 1–62.

13 Herriot, *Down from the Ivory Tower.*

10
Choosing selection methods

Having acquired a manageable pool of applicants, it is necessary to choose the best method or methods for making optimum selection decisions. This inevitably involves a compromise between accuracy, administrative convenience, and cost. Again it is a case of getting out what you put in. Many references have been made to selection methods in previous chapters. It is now necessary to consider the pros and cons more systematically.

Range of methods

This stretches from the cheapest and most easily administered method of random selection, through application forms, references, interviews, and standardized testing, to the costly and difficult to administer multi-method group selection. Unfortunately, there is a tendency for the range of accuracy to go in the opposite direction. The problem of striking a balance between cost and accuracy is aggravated by the range being from more accurate to less accurate rather than from totally accurate to totally inaccurate. Thus, to adopt the principle that it must be worthwhile developing the most sophisticated selection method available because, as discussed in Chapter 2, the cost of bad selection is very high, can be challenged on the grounds that extra trouble and expenditure may only produce a marginal improvement in accuracy.

There is also a tendency, by some selectors, to value predictive validity, in the statistical sense, over selection accuracy. That is, they seek to demonstrate that one aspect of a candidate will predict one part of the job performance with extreme precision, rather than considering what the whole person will make of the whole job. For this reason, and also to provide for fuller understanding of this chapter, it is important that the nature of prediction (Chapter 3) and the psychological attributes of candidates (Chapter 4) are appreciated.

Selection methods now need to be considered. They are discussed individually, but it must be remembered that it is the rule rather than the exception that a selection procedure will involve more than one.

Random selection

It may seem strange to include this as a selection method, as it almost appears by definition not to be one. It refers to the practice of deliberately refusing to use any degree of sophistication in selection on the grounds that it is just not cost-effective. In practice, what it means is that if all the applicants have the same qualifications and/or experience then we might as well apply the rule 'first come, first served'. The successful candidate is then simply informed of the result. In terms of the ratio of administrative ease to accuracy, this approach has actually got more going for it than many involved in selection would be happy to admit.

When should random selection be used? It is not really advocated, but it might be an efficient way of selecting either unqualified or very highly qualified temporary staff such as kitchen porters and deputizing doctors or dentists.

Application forms

The application form, or as it is sometimes referred to, the application blank, provides the major source of biographical data upon which selection decisions can be taken. The case can be made that this is the most under-used resource in the whole of selection. Candidates are being asked to complete what is, in essence, a questionnaire about themselves. Further, there are pressures on the candidate to complete this question-naire with some degree of honesty as they are often never quite sure what other sources of information the potential employer is likely to have and, for many candidates, the last thing they want to happen is to be caught out telling lies. As mentioned in the previous chapter, application form data have been shown to be reliable. This potentially rich source of information is often spoilt by organizations habitually using standardized and often dated application form designs. Forms are still to be found that ask applicants for all jobs to give details of their military/national service. Ideally, an application form should be perti-nent to the job being recruited for. A selector should ask the question 'What questionnaire data are going to be useful to me in order to help me make the selection decision for this job?' It should be borne in mind that an applicant is unlikely to offer more information than the space on the form permits. If we consider the example of selecting for the post of Office Manager, then it is useful if the application form not only provides space for applicants to list their previous jobs, but there is additional space for them to list the duties and responsibilities in some detail of any previous office management jobs that they may have held. Organizations defend the repeated use of the same application form on the grounds that it is tedious, time-consuming and sometimes costly to repeatedly redesign the form. However, with the development of word processors and sophisticated office reprographic facilities, the task has become considerably easier. If this is not possible, then at least the selector should examine the company's standardized application form and be aware in advance of the shortcomings of the data that it is likely to produce, and possibly add to it a supplementary sheet. A common compromise is to have available a range of standardized forms for different levels of job within the organization, for example school-leavers, graduates, hourly paid staff, salaried staff, and senior managerial staff. The form for school-leavers could request details of experience on government sponsored youth training schemes; the form for senior managerial staff would allow space for considerable detail on managerial experience.

It is difficult to prescribe good or bad application form design because this is dependent on the purpose for which they are being used. However, the design must allow, at least, for the following:

1   Candidates should be definitely identified – this requires full name and date of birth. Surname, initials and age alone are not enough when dealing with large numbers.

2   Candidates must be contactable – just asking for an address may disguise that there is both a permanent and temporary address, both of which should be noted; undergraduates, for example, are usually in this position.

3   Availability to attend for interview (or whatever is the next stage of the procedure) should be noted – this will make scheduling much easier.

4   Candidates should be asked to identify for which post or posts they are actually applying – it is not unknown for applicants to be rejected for jobs that they are not applying for. This is because they have not been given the chance to specify the job they are seeking.

5   A wide spectrum of education type – there are many routes to specific educational attainment levels. The form must allow for this, for example Scottish school-leavers can have difficulty fitting their qualifications under the headings of 'O' levels and 'A' levels.

6   The meaning of 'interests' should be unambiguous – if these are asked for, does it mean leisure or work interests or both? Is it just hobbies? Should it include posts held in organizations related to leisure pursuits, etc? – this should be specified.

7   The meaning of 'experience' should be unambiguous – does this mean previous jobs held, or the skills that an applicant considers he or she has? – this should be specified.

8   Ethnic monitoring – under the Code of Practice issued by the Commission for Racial Equality (see Chapter 5), employers are recommended to include on application forms explicit questions

related to ethnic origin.[1] This is to allow ethnic monitoring to be carried out.

9 Return of completed forms – it should be made very clear where and to whom in the organization the candidate should send the completed application form.

10 Processing of application form data should be considered – if a systematic form of pre-selection is being used which involves scoring on the actual form itself, then a blank margin should be provided and the candidate requested to leave it blank. If records are being kept by personnel departments of key information held on application forms, especially of the successful applicants, then this should be easily extractable, for example design the application form so that these important data appear all on the same page.

Many forms, especially those for higher level jobs, contain a mixture of direct, closed instructions to elicit specific information – for example 'Please list your educational qualifications with dates' – and open-ended instructions – for example 'Please use this page to add any information you feel will benefit your application'. The latter can provide some useful insights into the candidate. This is particularly true if the application form is being evaluated as a document that represents how a candidate sees himself or herself at the time of applying and how he or she sees fit to put that over.[2] But there are dangers inherent in the use of this form of self-assessment. If few guidelines are provided as to how these parts of the form are to be completed, then the candidate who knows what answers will give the 'right impression' scores an advantage over the one who answers frankly and honestly. A fairly recent study of how 118 final-year undergraduates responded to open-ended sections of application forms has provided a number of suggestions as to the ways in which form designers can deal with this problem.[3] They are:

- Requests for self-assessment of complex characteristics should be kept to a minimum.

- The emphasis should not be on future aspirations.

- The need for indirect approaches. It is better to request that responses be about past behaviour and experiences, and it is the selector who should draw inferences about personal characteristics.

- Guidelines given to the applicants should point them towards potentially relevant experiences.

- Guidance should be given, on the form, on how to analyse important experiences.

- Some closed format questions could usefully be converted to an open format. Those relating to academic performance are a case in point.

- Different types of job require different open-ended questions. Note: the study found that undergraduates from different discipline areas responded in a particular way.

- There should be considerable interchange of information between form designers and applicants, as users.

The application form is an important selection tool. It can influence decisions even at the final stages of selection. Another study of graduate selection has indicated that judgements of candidates made by scanning the form correlate $r = 0.40$ with judgements made after the interview.[4]

When should application forms be used? In almost every case, especially if screening is to take place. It is difficult to think of a situation when this inexpensive and efficient source of information is not useful. That is, as long as it is designed for the job in question.

It is not particularly useful in those cases where applicants lack sufficient skills to complete it, but ability to communicate in this way is not a part of the job. Indeed using application forms which demand a certain level of language ability which the job does not require can result in illegal discrimination.[5]

References

Under this heading must be included a whole range of formal and informal contacts between selectors and other organizations. Some of these could be grouped together as the use of 'the old boy network'. This constitutes a rather unusual phenomenon which is worth commenting on. While it is a method of selection which many organizations would not be happy to admit to, and which is frequently held in contempt, it is one which selectors informally but frequently validate. Selectors and managers will have a range of friends and acquaintances who are willing to give a candid, normally verbal, opinion of a mutually known candidate, or who can put you in touch with someone who can. If, however, the information provided by someone in the network turns out to be seriously misleading, then it is likely that that individual would be jettisoned as a future source of information, unlike misleading information that might be provided in a selection test or interview, which would be written off as just bad luck.

More normally, the practice of taking up references refers to a formal approach to an applicant's previous employer. The attitude to references is rather like that to astrology, in as much as there is public cynicism but some degree of private belief. On the one hand, selectors know they must not rely on reference data, but, on the other, they find it hard not to be influenced by it. Unlike the 'old boy network', which, because of its rather clandestine characteristics, is rarely evaluated, the use of the formal reference has to some extent been investigated. The evidence produced indicates that the public cynicism is justified. One rather dated but still frequently cited study,[6] which looked at references supplied for over 1000 applicants for US Civil Service posts, found:

1 Less than 1 per cent were given poor references on either ability or character.

2 Approximately 50 per cent were given 'outstanding' references.

3 In answer to a question asking whether the applicant was especially qualified for the job, those given 'no' by the referees turned out to be no worse than those given 'yes', with the exception of painters, where the 'no's did in fact perform slightly better.

A much more recent review concerning the usefulness of references[7] offers little to change this rather disappointing picture. One glimmer of hope has, however, been provided.[8] It was found that a reasonable correlation ($r = 0.64$) existed between the present and previous employer's assessment of the employee, but what was used in this case was a highly structured rating form using a forced choice format and the following conditions:

1 The referee has adequate time to observe the employee working.

2 The referee from the old job is from the same sex, race and nationality as the employee.

3 The old job and the new job are very similar in content.

In summary, it would seem that references are in reality of little help in selection. If one is going to be used then it should be carefully designed and highly structured and not simply an open-ended request for general comments and observations. Even then it should only be seen as providing vague supplementary data to those collected in other parts of the selection procedure. They are grossly under-researched and therefore under-developed.[9] These reservations about the value of references apply when they are being used to assess such things as ability and personality. Clearly references are of value when they are to seek information which can be objectively assessed by the referee, such as confirmation of the applicant's job title, length of service, and attendance record.

When should references be used? Only in those situations where there is a danger that candidates may misrepresent their actual identity and that of their previous job, and this cannot be verified by other selection methods.

The selection interview

Since W. D. Scott, as early as 1915, identified the selection interview to be rather less than adequate as a dependable selection method, there have been many subsequent investigations. These have largely focused on the free-flowing unstructured type of event that normally characterizes this selection method, and have been evaluated from time to time in review articles, all of which, including the most recent,[10] offer no strong reason to alter this view. Much of the research has sought to impose a scientific evaluation on this ill-defined practice. It is thus concerned with its reliability and validity: is it a stable measure of people, and can it predict job performance (see Chapter 3)? The reliability is generally found to be dubious and the validity very disappointing and suspect. One review politely concluded: 'Reported reliabilities are lower than usually accepted for devices used for individual prediction and therefore unreliability remains a serious source of attenuation for any validity coefficients which might be found.'[11] Nevertheless it remains the most widely practised method of selection. Further, it has been suggested that its stubbornness in refusing to go away makes it arguably an increasingly interesting phenomenon to investigate.[12] The question must therefore be asked: 'With so much evidence stacked against it, why does the selection interview still survive?' Possible explanations, which by their very nature are interrelated, might be:

1   The meaning of 'validity'. Most research has used this term in a narrow sense to mean that something that is measurable is able to predict something else that is measurable and that the prediction itself is measurable (for example, using correlation coefficients). There is a justification for the interview, if the term is more broadly interpreted. The interview may be 'valid' as in the example of a manager who claims, 'As I have got to work closely with this employee I need an interview to judge whether we are going to get on together'. Given this statement, it would be hard to justify the avoidance of an interview in selection.

2   The role of judgemental prediction. As was discussed in Chapter 3, the use of judgemental or clinical prediction in selection must be given serious consideration. This relies on the complex exchange of data between selector and candidate, which requires personal contact. The form of this is normally the interview.

3   The recruitment function. The interview is clearly an ideal opportunity for the organization to sell itself to the candidate and provide a very effective way of easily meeting the candidate's need for information.

4   The interview as ritual. Both employers and candidates have an expectation that there ought to be an interview, almost regardless of whether it is actually helping the selection process. If a candidate is offered a job without interview, he or she often feels denied something that they are entitled to, even though the ultimate goal has been achieved. It is almost as if the interview constitutes the *rites de passage* of entry into the organization.

5 Uselessness of research evidence. A reason for ignoring the scientific caveat offered to the interviewer is the destructive rather than constructive nature of the evidence. The research, while condemning conventional interview practices, has attempted to provide pointers to how the process can be improved. Unfortunately, these attempts have not been particularly fruitful, especially in developing a body of knowledge as a basis for interviewer training.[13] Much of the research has been laboratory-based, and this has been commented upon by one reviewer thus: 'The generalizability of these artificial and microanalytic studies to real employment situations remains unestablished.'[14]

These reasons, which are offered to explain the continuing popularity of the selection interview, must not be taken as a negation of the scientific evidence. The case made by W. D. Scott and his scientific successors must not be ignored by selectors.

Types of selection interview

Whether selection interviewers should carry out their tasks as a group, or panel, sequentially, or individually, is the sort of issue referred to above, about which there is conflicting evidence.[15] The choice of the most suitable type of interview to use needs to be based largely on considerations other than predictive validity.

The board interview

A justification frequently offered for the board interview is that it reduces biased decision-making. The interviewee's behaviour is being observed by more than one person, which can avoid the extreme interpretation of that behaviour that one interviewer might make. It should follow logically from this that the larger the board, the less likelihood there will be of extreme judgements. There is, however, little research evidence to support this. Interview boards do not make significantly better decisions than individual interviewers.[16]

One of the reasons for this is that at interview boards have to come to an agreed decision. The process of reaching that decision introduces the variable of a group dynamic within the board. In practice, this raises the issue: does each member have an equal say in the final decision? For example, where a board has a chairperson who is a very much more senior member of the organization than the rest of the board, it is quite likely that his or her opinion is a major influence on the selection decision. Alternatively, a board member with a particularly aggressive or forthright personality may also disproportionately influence the board's decision.

A further possible explanation why this type of interview is not seen to be more valid is that the candidate, by virtue of being outnumbered, finds it difficult to see the encounter as an informal chat. The result is that the interview takes on a mantle of restrictive formality, which can get in the way of a genuine exchange of real feelings and beliefs.[17]

A second rationale for the board interview is a political one – that is it is sometimes unwise to exclude certain interested parties from taking part in this stage of the selection. In fact, in many organizations, the constitution of interview boards is mandatory, described in terms of post titles not post holders. An example is the case of certain teacher appointments, where the employing Local Authority insists that the interview is conducted by a board consisting of the Head Teacher, the Chairman of the Board of Governors, a nominee of the Education Officer, and at least two members of the Authority's Education Committee. Their place on the board is a function of their status not of their ability to carry out a selection interview.

It must be pointed out that, while the board interview appears to be no better than a single interview, there is nothing to say that it is a lot worse. If political considerations are important within the organization, then this is probably enough to justify this method of interviewing, that is as long as the board is of manageable size (this usually means four or less) and each member knows what his or her role is during the interview. This means that there should be an agreed chairperson, and how members should function in their roles should be discussed in advance.

The single interview

The advantages and disadvantages of the single interview are the opposite of those for the board interview. There is no check on interview bias, but it does allow a climate of trust and openness to be developed. This latter point is important as recent articles have suggested that this is the direction that research on interviewing will have to go in order to improve the efficiency of this selection method. This is likely to enhance the status of the single interview.[18]

The sequential interview

This is where a number of interviewers see each candidate, not as a board, but separately. While it is an expensive and time-consuming attempt at a compromise between the two other interview types, it allows interviewers to build up a relationship with the interviewee and can meet the political demands of the selection process. However, it is often unpopular with non-specialist interviewers, and still requires a group decision. But it does allow for a procedure whereby each interviewer independently makes their decision about a candidate, which gives some indication of the consensus, uncontaminated by the power and influence within the selecting group. As a compromise, sequential interviewing is more than satisfactory. As an aid to selection it has the slight edge over the other two approaches.[19]

Undertaking an interview

To attempt to impart interviewing skills through a book of this nature is as appropriate as trying to improve someone's golf performance in the same way. It is possible to become familiar with certain basic 'rules', but to become skilled in the necessary behaviour requires feedback on performance that can best be gained from a training programme as described in Chapter 6; thus, this section is devoted to considering these basic rules.

Rule 1: *Have an objective*

Before undertaking an interview, the interviewer should decide why he or she is doing it. What do they want to get out of it? It will be different for every candidate. The job and person specification will tell you the information that you will want by the end of the interview. Application forms, references, etc., will give you information before you start. Thus, the interview time should be spent investigating the difference between the information you need and what you have already got. In other words, each interview needs some prior planning. It needs to be custom-built to the applicant. Careful attention to this stage prevents time-wasting by the interviewer, such as simply reading out the application form and making such statements as 'I see that you . . .', to which the candidate replies accurately but unhelpfully 'Yes'. The labels of 'personnel' and 'technical' are often applied to describe the difference between an interview that focuses on personality and interests and one that concerns itself with ability. Those who carry out these interviews often worry about keeping within their own 'territory', never really knowing where the boundary is. However, if, for example, the personnel specialist, on the one hand, and the technical manager, on the other, simply set their objectives in line with what they feel they would like to get out of the given interview, the boundary issue would not exist. In other words, these labels have no meaning. It is just that different interviewers involved in the process have different objectives.

Rule 2: *Make a contract*

This is the practice whereby the interviewer outlines to the candidate how he is going to proceed during the interview, presenting what is almost an agenda and getting the candidate to agree. This might take the following form:

> 'What I would like to do, Mr Smith, during the next three-quarters of an hour, is to explore your reasons for applying, look at your occupational history, consider your educational background, especially the peaks and troughs, and

find out a little bit about you in terms of how you spend your spare time, and obviously I will do my best to answer any questions that you might have – is that OK with you?'

Most interviewees will say 'Yes', but the exceptional case who challenges the agenda is indicating a strength of feeling about this interview which must be brought to the surface and dealt with in order for the interview to have a chance of achieving anything. Two further advantages of the contract are, firstly, interviewees feel that they have been consulted about the design of the process, which can put them at ease much more effectively than a lengthy list of apparently insincere pleasantries, and, secondly, it enables the interviewer to say, later on, 'Well, as we agreed at the beginning, Mr Smith, I would now like to go on and look at how you spend your spare time', and similar phrases that can help the interview to move on.

Rule 3: *Take control*
The interview should belong to the interviewer. It is he or she who decides in which direction it needs to go in order to meet the original objective. If control is allowed to pass to the interviewee then, as a selection device, it is likely to become even more random than it would otherwise be. The interviewer should operate a number of control devices, two of these are worth mentioning here.

1   *Summaries*   As a matter of course an interviewer should summarize, at the end of the interview, the picture that he has got of the candidate, so that information can be verified and added to. Also summaries should appear during the interview as and when necessary, the normal reason being for the interviewer to assess the information that has been given. That embarrassing silence when the interviewer is saying to himself 'I am not quite sure what to ask about next' can usefully be filled by the phrase 'I would just like to take stock of the picture that I am getting of you at the moment'. The ensuing summary gives valuable thinking time and creates an impression of competence and interest.

2   *Questioning techniques*   Many guides to interviewing skills have long lists of labels to describe different types of questions. Basically the interviewer needs to be aware of three: firstly, there is the leading question. This is where the interviewer influences the answer by the way the question is asked, for example 'You are not going to find any difficulty in adjusting to a company of this size are you?' Awareness of this question type is important in order to avoid it. It contaminates the information that is received from the candidate. Secondly, there is the open question. This is the sort of question that is difficult to answer briefly. It encourages the interviewee to speak, providing their own structures for the answer,

for example 'Tell me what you think the differences are in working in a company of this size?' The open question generates the data on which the interviewer must work. It provides the essential raw material for the interview. Thirdly, there is the closed question. This is a question which invites a more precise, limited answer – questions that ask for 'Yes', or 'No' or Where? When? How many? etc., for example, 'How many weeks do you think it will take to sell your house?' While the open question generates information, the closed question checks it out. A crude rule of thumb in selection interviewing is that each major part of the interview should begin with a series of open questions, followed by a probing series of closed questions.

Rule 4: *Always listen*
It is impossible to control an interview if the interviewer is not listening. On the one hand, this involves the skill of actually being able to retain a lot of information – an exercise for the short-term memory. In the space of even half an hour a candidate can provide a great deal of information. The interviewer has to retain it in order to use it, relate it, and check for inconsistencies at different times during the interview. The simple skill of remembering information can be improved by practising it.

On the other hand, listening can refer to the ability to be sensitive to what the interviewee is meaning rather than just to what he or she is saying. It is the ability to listen to more than words. For example, an applicant asked about his or her previous job might reply 'It was OK'. Those words, depending on how they are said, can convey anything from 'I found it extremely enjoyable' to 'I did not enjoy it but I put up with it'. An interviewer needs to be aware that he has to interpret that quality of data.

Rule 5: *Interviews should be structured*
There is evidence suggesting that in the freee-flowing interview the reliability increases if a consistent structure is used.[20] This obviously does not mean a standard set of questions which is universally applicable to all candidates, although that is what many interviewers would like to have. It refers to a kind of template that is metaphorically placed over the information about the candidate during the objective-setting or planning stage referred to above. It is a set of questions about aspects of the candidate that the interviewer must ask in order to decide where to concentrate his efforts during the interview. Probably the most widely used British schema has been Rodger's Seven-Point Plan, which had a considerable influence on the design of the Job Analysis Checklist described in Chapter 7. The part of the JAC labelled 'person specification' can be used as an interviewing structure.

*

These 'rules' have omitted items which many may consider important, such as physical environment, note-taking and interviewer posture. In fact, they are not omitted but implicitly contained. It is dangerous to be prescriptive about whether an interviewer should sit behind a desk or sit with the interviewee in easy chairs, etc. Basically, at the planning stage of the interview, the interviewer should ask himself where he will feel the most comfortable. Clearly, it is likely to be counter-productive if, in the name of informality, an interviewer is forced to sit in an easy chair to conduct the interview, which is a situation that he or she is ill at ease with.

The degree of listening skill that an interviewer has obviously dictates the extent of note-taking which is necessary. Even if this is quite excessive it can be comfortably dealt with as an item on the 'agenda' at the contract stage.

As all of the above applies to the common, relatively unstructured, interview, it is important to compare it with the somewhat different 'situational interview' which grew in popularity in the 1980s.[21]

This procedure involves the use of predetermined questions, often directly based on job analysis and demonstrably job related. The interviewer asks the same questions of all the interviewees.

Under these conditions reliability is much improved,[22] with validity showing an ever more dramatic increase.[23] However, two important points must be made. Firstly, validated predetermined questions suggest the need for prescriptive answers to be offered in an interview situation. This practice may well be challengeable on equal opportunity grounds. Secondly, the situational interview can become little more than a spoken ability test. As such it can prove a much costlier exercise than its written counterpoint.

In summary, the interview as a selection device is the most widely used, largely because it is the most difficult to dispose of. It suffers from a distinct lack of precision in predicting subsequent job performance, but has the advantage of being much more embracing than other selection methods, and provides the rich interpersonal data that allow clinical or judgemental decisions to be made. While most selection methods seek to answer the question 'Has the applicant the ability to do the job?', the interview can provide clues to answer the question 'Does the candidate really want to do this job?'.

When should interviews be used? It is easier to address the question of when should they not be used? Because they provide just about the only selection method for identifying the applicant's real commitment to the job, they are usually essential, but if this is not a major concern, then they could become a costly, ineffective appendage to the selection procedure. If the selection decision requires narrow but accurate predictive information about subsequent job performance, then the interview will not provide this. For example, it may only have a minor role to play in the selection of scarce but very highly skilled staff. The interview is an attractive selection method for the small employer as costs are normally directly proportional to the number of applicants, unlike other methods which are at their most expensive with small numbers.

Selection testing

This method provides recruitment and selection with an overlay of scientific respectability. It isolates the psychological dimensions of a candidate and attempts to accurately measure them. It is a frequently misunderstood and abused selection method because of failure to understand what testing involves, especially at a theoretical level. This has been discussed at some length in Chapters 3 and 4, which means it is unnecessary to re-open that discussion here, other than to emphasize some of the major points.

Testing is essentially an attempt to achieve objectivity, or, to put it more accurately, to reduce subjectivity in selection decision-making. If undertaken correctly, it can narrowly measure aspects of a candidate relatively accurately. This can only be achieved if the test is valid. This is in addition to it being standardized, sensitive and reliable. In practical terms, it means that a selector should not use a test unless he or she is satisfied with its demonstrated validity, which is usually expressed as the coefficient of correlation between test performance and some measure of subsequent job performance.

The real danger of selection testing is that it often looks more accurate than it actually is. Like so many mechanistic devices to aid human judgement, inaccuracies are not evident during the period of use, but only manifest themselves when it is too late. As an illustration, we can take the analogy of the gun-sight of a rifle. In the case of it being inaccurate, the inexperienced user will assume that, because the sight is there, it is accurate, and will be totally influenced by the information that the gun-sight provides. If the gun is reliable, then logic dictates that the user must miss the target. Hopefully, he will then realize that the validity of the instrument he is using is in question, and stop using the gun until he is satisfied that the gun-sight has been corrected to give accuracy. If he is reluctant to give up firing the gun, he might justify that it has accuracy by always defining the target as that which he actually hits – a reckless and dangerous prospect. With the gun-sight as the selection test, and the shot as the selection decision, the implication is that many selectors confidently use tests without questioning their validity, and modify their selection decisions in order to justify continued use of the test.

In short, the real danger of testing is that the confidence inspired by its apparent objectivity can be seriously abused.

On the assumption that we are referring to responsibly-operated testing, as a selection method it offers both advantages and disadvantages.

Testing in general

Advantages
1   Predictive validity can be demonstrated in statistical terms for certain candidate attributes.
2   Most selection tests are of a pencil and paper variety, and therefore candidates can be tested in groups – it is normally recommended that one tester can handle fifteen to twenty applicants in one 'sitting'.
3   Inexpensive to use after purchase of re-usable testing materials.

Disadvantages
1   Cannot measure the entire candidate, which causes gaps in the valid information for making decisions.
2   Where tests are used to measure the psychological attributes of the candidate, then a knowledge of psychology is necessary to interpret the test result.
3   Initial purchase of re-usable materials can be costly.
4   Those administering and interpreting tests may need special training.

Attainment testing
(For example, typing speed and accuracy tests, final examinations of professional bodies)

Advantages
1   Provides a dependable measure of the candidate's minimal level of skill.
2   Useful in jobs where no training is to be given, especially in technical areas.

Disadvantages
1   Does not indicate candidate's typical level of performance.
2   Danger of generalizing on actual performance measured, for example a typist who successfully copies a business letter as a typing attainment test will not necessarily be able to type other sorts of documents with equal success.

Aptitude testing
(For example, computer programming aptitude tests, language ability tests, verbal reasoning tests, mechanical reasoning tests)

Advantages
1 Lessens the subjective error in assessing a candidate's potential to develop a job-related aptitude.
2 Often very easy to administer.

Disadvantages
1 The tests are designed to measure only a defined aptitude and therefore do not relate to additional aspects of job performance.
2 The ease of administration belies the difficulty in interpretation.

Personality measurement
(For example, personality trait questionnaires, prospective techniques using such stimuli as 'ink blots', assessments of group membership behaviour, some leadership style questionnaires)

Advantages
1 Allows the quantification of characteristics which are very important to job performance and are difficult to measure by other methods.
2 Easy to administer and often entertaining for the candidate.

Disadvantages
1 Very difficult to interpret results requiring a high level of expertise, and thus very easily abused.
2 Very difficult to formally validate within a selection procedure.
3 Sometimes disapproved of by candidates and trade unions as being irrelevant.
4 Answers are fakable, especially in a selection context.
5 Much current debate about their true worth.

Interest measurement
(For example, occupational interest questionnaires)

Advantages
1 Gives some indication of a candidate's inclinations rather than just capacities.
2 Sometimes useful if the results are used as discussion points within a selection interview.

Disadvantages
1 Very difficult to use as a valid predictor of job performance.
2 The problem of faking renders it unsuitable for selection decision-making, unless treated with extreme caution.

Testing is a useful selection method when narrow, but precise information is required. This is particularly true in the case of ability, but there is the danger that the degree of precision can be overestimated. Surveys have indicated that a selector will be doing quite well if the test that he is using correlates more than r = 0.4 with subsequent job performance.[24]

Multiple-method group selection

Up to this point the discussion on selection methods has tended to treat each method separately. In reality, selection is likely to involve a combination of several methods, based on a desire for accuracy, tempered by administrative cost and convenience. The normal practice is for each candidate to be subjected to these compounded assessment methods. If each of these methods is considered to have some predictive value in its own right, then the selector is faced with the problems of multiple prediction as discussed in Chapter 3. Exceptionally, some organizations, usually large ones, use group selection methods. Instead of assessing individual candidates one at a time through the selection procedure, they will form them into groups and assess them in that group. Long-standing examples are the selection of officers in the British Army and the selection for administration grades in the British Civil Service. This kind of selection has three essential features in addition to the use of the candidate group.

1   A wide range of selection techniques is used.

2   Assessment is carried out by a group of judges.

3   The procedure as a whole is validated.

This is the 'assessment centre' approach which was mentioned in Chapter 3. Its use is normally found in the assessment of candidates for managerial positions. It can take up several days of the candidate's time.

Range of techniques

The method works on the principle that candidates should be subjected to a wide range of selection techniques or methods. Individually, these have a limited but positive validity. Collectively, they will produce data that can be converted into a useful predictor of job performance. Thus, the following could be considered to be typical.

Firstly, there are the conventional selection methods, namely the use of biographical questionnaires, interviews and psychological tests, the last of these consisting of both ability tests and personality questionnaires.

Secondly, there is the use of the 'group discussion', which is a technique whereby the candidates sit down together and are given a topic to discuss. The assessors, who do not appoint a leader to the group, remain outside, observing the ensuing interaction. This appears to be an effective procedure for measuring such dimensions as oral expression, interpersonal skills, and influence, etc.[25]

The topics should be carefully chosen to maximize the interaction between group members. Each should meet the following requirements:

- It must not require specialist knowledge that favours individuals in the group.

- It should relate to an issue about which candidates are likely to have strong views.

- Early consensus of opinion is unlikely.

The discussion can be assessed in an unstructured way with assessors being asked to make any comment they wish on the group member's behaviour that they have observed. A loose structure can be imposed where assessment relates to such questions as 'Does the group member get his ideas across?', 'Does he appear to influence other members' thinking?' or 'Does he dictate the direction that the discussion should go?'. In contrast, a highly structured classification of verbal utterances can be used. One such long-established approach utilizes the following categories: shows solidarity; shows tension; release; agrees; gives suggestions; gives opinions; gives orientation; asks for orientation; asks for opinions; asks for suggestions; disagrees; shows tension; and shows antagonism.[26] Members can be compared by counting the number of times they exhibit behaviour under each of these categories.

Thirdly, there are work-simulation exercises. At a macro-level, business games are used. Often the candidate group is divided into smaller competing teams. These games, which are frequently computer-based, can indicate, to observers, leadership ability in a business context, and more general business sense.

At the micro-level, a common technique is an 'in-tray exercise'. It involves group members individually being confronted with the same in-tray containing a pile of simulated management problems in the form of paperwork which the candidate has to deal with. How he or she performs is observed and group members are compared. These exercises should be designed so that they can be objectively marked by assessors. This technique is a useful way of seeing how the candidate will perform under job pressure and how rational their decision-making is.[27]

Assessment by judges

The assessment centre in selection, while containing statistical devices such as psychological tests, is essentially a judgemental/clinical method. It capitalizes on the number and experience of assessors, who are normally senior managers assisted by psychologists, all having been trained in the skills of assessment. It would be typical to have one assessor to every two or three candidates in the group. Each assessor carefully observes part of the group at each stage of the process. The role of the judges is to reach some consensus at the end of the few days on each candidate's rating against the job requirement.

Validating the whole procedure

What differentiates assessment centre group selection from the simple compounding of selection methods is that the whole activity should be validated as a single method, that is the final decision of the judges is the predictor of job success. Much validity information has been accumulated during the 1980s which indicates that it is one of the best ways of predicting job success.[28]

This kind of group selection has an additional advantage of having very high face validity. It looks like just the sort of procedure you need to sort out who are going to make good managers and who are not. This is, of course, a mixed blessing. A major disadvantage of this form of selection is that it is horrendously expensive, largely because of the time taken in preparation and development, assessor training and running the actual assessment. It is for this reason that, desirable though this method may be, it is limited to the large and wealthy employers.

When should multi-method group selection be used? Disregarding cost, the assessment centre is the best selection method. If key members of an organization are to be selected, for example senior managers, then the selection decision will have to be correct. This method must be considered. It is also viable when selecting less senior staff, as long as there is a large 'through-put' of candidates. This, at least, spreads the development costs of the assessment centre.

When an assessment centre is being used to assess internal candidates, care should be taken on two counts.

Firstly, the situation where some of the assessors have special or unique prior knowledge of some of the candidates should be avoided if possible.

Secondly, personnel files which may contain performance appraisal reports should not be consulted until after the assessors have made their final decision. To do otherwise is to introduce a measure from outside the validated procedure of the assessment centre.

If the group consists of both internal and external candidates, even greater care must be taken.

While this method is the best, it is not perfect. Thus, there is the inherent danger that it might be used as a 'sledgehammer to crack a nut'.

Other selection methods

Brief consideration is given here to other, perhaps less orthodox, methods of selection.

- Graphology. On the face of it the analysis of handwriting appears to be a worthwhile selection method to pursue. It certainly provides the stamp of an individual. It is recognizably idiosyncratic. However, despite recent increased public interest in this method reviewers of rigorous research are forced to conclude that there is virtually no empirical evidence to suggest that it accurately predicts job performance.[29]

- Palmistry. While this practice as a method of assessing individual traits is usually reliable, inexpensive and cannot be damaged by faking, selectors are unlikely to gain anything of great value from it.

- Astrology. Certainly, as things stand, astrology has nothing to offer those involved in recruitment and selection, but, before it is dismissed totally out of hand, it should be noted that the work of the Gauquelins in France and Eysenck in Britain has caused some surprise and eyebrows to be raised because of the impressive statistical analyses provided.

When should these 'other' methods be used? Not at all at present. There is no evidence to support them as worthwhile.

Choosing between selection methods

It has been indicated above that each selection method has its advantages and disadvantages. In reality, understanding these can cause nearly as many problems for the selector as it solves. How are these balanced to provide the optimum selection procedure for filling a post or posts? The answer depends on the size of the company, budgets available, numbers of applicants, need for accuracy, and, of course, the nature of the job itself.

It may be useful to the selector, in the designing of a procedure to meet his or her needs, to approach it systematically in the following way:

1 Draw up a matrix, with the selection methods listed on the horizontal, and the items from the person specification of the job analysis checklist (see Chapter 7) on the vertical.

2 Consider each cell of the matrix in terms of the value that a selection method will have in assessing that aspect of the person being sought for the job in question.

3 Apply some scoring system (for example '10' for 'will assess it perfectly' down to '1' for 'will not assess it at all').

4   Vertical columns with the highest numbers will indicate the most suitable combination of selection methods. These need to be then assessed against cost.

Perhaps the final act is to step back and view the selection method scenario for what it can offer. The most sophisticated methods known to humankind can only ever hope to predict 35 per cent to 45 per cent of someone's ability to do the job. Whilst this is, of course, very useful, the rest is still left to chance.[30]

Summary

To those involved in selection there is a range of methods available. Choosing the methods to use for any given selection task is not only a function of the job being selected for, but also involves costs and need for accuracy. Application forms are extremely efficient at collecting important biographical data, but they must be designed properly. References have little to recommend them. The selection interview, be it a board, single, or sequential type, is not as effective at predicting job performance as its popularity might suggest, but it produces a breadth of data which it is difficult to manage without.

Selection testing can predict narrow aspects of the job performance, and for some appointments this is the primary concern. However it is the 'assessment centre' approach which produces the best overall prediction. But it is the most expensive method.

Other methods such as graphology, palmistry and astrology have little to offer.

References

1   *Code of Practice for the elimination of racial discrimination and the promotion of equality of opportunity in employment*, Commission for Racial Equality (1983).

2   P. Herriot, *Down From the Ivory Tower* (Wiley 1984).

3   A. Keenan, 'Where application forms mislead', *Personnel Management* (January 1983), p. 40–3.

4   P. Herriot and C. Rothwell, 'Expectations and impressions in the graduate selection interview', *Journal of Occupational Psychology*, **56** (1983).

5   *Code of Practice*, Commission for Racial Equality.

6   J. N. Mosel and H. W. Goheen, 'The validity of the employment recommendation questionnaire in personnel selection', *Personnel Psychology*, **2** (1958), p. 487–90.

7   P. M. Muchinsky, 'The use of reference reports in personnel selection. A review and evaluation', *Journal of Occupational Psychology*, **52** (1979), p. 287–97.

8   S. J. Carroll and A. N. Nash, 'Effectiveness of a force-choice reference check', *Personnel Administration*, **35** (1972), p. 42–6.

9   P. Dobson, 'Reference Reports', in P. Herriot (ed.) *Assessment and Selection in Organisations* (Wiley 1989).

10 M. M. Harris, 'Reconsidering the employment interview: a review of recent literature and suggestions for future research', *Personnel Psychology*, **42** (1989), p. 691–726.

11 L. Ulrich and D. Trumbo, 'The selection interview since 1949', *Psychological Bulletin*, **63** (1965), p. 100–16.

12 C. Lewis, 'Investigating the employment interview', *Journal of Occupational Psychology*, **53** (1980), p. 111–16.

13 C. Lewis, 'The use of research findings in interview training', paper to the Annual Occupational Psychology Conference (Warwick, January 1983).

14 N. Schmidt, 'Social and situational determinants of interview decisions: Implications for the employment interview', *Personnel Psychology*, **29** (1976), p. 79–101.

15 Lewis, 'The use of research findings in interview training'.

16 R. Bayne, C. Fletcher and J. Colwell, 'Board and sequential interviews in selection: An experimental study of their comparative effectiveness', *Personnel Review*, **12** (1983), p. 3, 14–19.

17 Lewis, 'Investigating the employment interview'.

18 R. D. Arvey and J. E. Campion, 'The Employment Interview: a summary and review of present research', *Personnel Psychology*, **35** (1982), p. 281–322.
Lewis, 'Investigating the employment interview'.

19 Bayne, Fletcher and Colwell, 'Board and sequential interviews in selection'.

20 E. C. Mayfield, 'The selection interview: A re-evaluation of published research', *Personnel Psychology*, **17** (1964), p. 239–60.

21 G. P. Latham, L. M. Saari, E. D. Pursell and M. A. Campion, 'The situational interview', *Journal of Applied Psychology*, **65** (1980), p. 422–

22 J. A. Weekley and J. A. Gier, 'Reliability and validity of the situational interview for a sales person', *Journal of Applied Psychology*, **72** (1987), p. 484–7.

23 W. H. Wiesner and S. F. Cronshaw, 'A meta-analytic investigation of the impact of interview format and degree of structure on the validity of the employment interview', *Journal of Occupational Psychology*, **61** (1988), p. 275–90.

24 E. E. Ghiselli, *The Validity of Occupational Aptitude Tests* (Wiley 1966).

25 B. M. Bass, 'The leaderless group discussion', *Psychological Bulletin*, **51** (1954), p. 465–92.

26 R. F. Bales, *Interaction Process Analysis* (Addison-Wesley 1950).

27 R. W. T. Gill, 'The in-tray exercise as a measure of management potential', *Journal of Occupational Psychology*, **52** (1979), p. 185–98.

28 B. B. Gaugler, D. B. Rosenthal, G. C. Thornton and C. Bentson, 'Meta-analysis of assessment center validity', *Journal of Applied Psychology*, **72** (1987), p. 493–511.

29 G. Ben-Shakhar, 'Non-conventional methods in Personnel Selection' in P. Herriot (ed.), *Assessment and Selection in Organisations* (Wiley 1989).

30 C. Lewis, 'Selection Methods and How to Cope With Them', in L. Rushbrook (ed.), *The Recruitment Guide* (CEPEC 1991).

11
Making selection decisions

Underlying the issues raised in Chapter 3 was the debate as to whether it is possible to develop a scientifically-based decision-making procedure that predicts future job performance or if, in the end, the choice of candidate depends upon human judgement. It would appear, in practice, that the best approach is to accept that human judgement will be used in the final decision, but that this will be aided by scientifically or statistically validated pieces of information, such as test results.

Unfortunately, systematic attempts to do this are hindered by the progressive use of selection methods. These become hurdles for the candidate to conquer, with rejection decisions being made by selectors at each. Candidates rejected at the first hurdle – for example, on the basis of an application form – have provided far less information for decision-making than those rejected at the last hurdle – for example, having been tested and having undergone several interviews, etc.

For this reason it is erroneous to attempt to design a sophisticated selection procedure which is made up of a large number of small hurdles. A small number of large hurdles would aid better decision-making. It should be administrative expediency only which prevents all candidates from going through the whole procedure up to the final selection decision. In practice, this means that final shortlists should be as long as possible to reduce selection errors.

There have been psychologists who, for many years, have concerned themselves with the phenomenon that human beings cannot cope with incomplete and ambiguous information and, if confronted with it, will add subjective data based on their own experience, prejudices or values, etc. This model has a relevance for selectors. It suggests that early, confident decision-making may occur because the selector makes assumptions which add to the objective data provided by the candidate. In other words, it explains why many selectors do not query their own readiness to make decisions simply on the basis of an application form, brief interview or test result. They believe they have more information than actually exists. The data are enriched by themselves. An illustration of the dangerous ease with which this can happen is an interviewer's comment such as 'I was very impressed by candidate X, but on paper I would not have thought he had a chance' – thus, this good candidate would have been lost by an early decision based on his application form.

Example 11.1 is an extract from a graduate recruitment application form of a large petrochemical company (the names have been changed).

Example 11.1 *Extract from a graduate recruitment application form*

Name	F. T. Pearson
Address	33 Swayling Road, Bradford, Yorks.
University	University of Bradford
Subject	Chemical Engineering
Class of degree expected	2:1 or 1st
Post applied for	Process Engineer
Interests	Reading, cricket, parachuting and motor cycling
University posts of responsibility	Member of Student Council
Career ambitions	To gain experience as an engineer and move into a managerial position in about eight years

---

A group of managers asked to comment on the applicant all assumed that the candidate was male – this was incorrect. The worrying aspect is, had they not been told of the candidate's sex and if she was the only female applicant, they may well have claimed, with a great deal of conviction, that 'no female process enginners had applied'. This brief example indicates that errors can occur almost below the threshold of awareness, that is selectors are often not sensitive to the limitations of their knowledge about a candidate.

Decision-making and the interview

The process by which interviewers reach decisions about candidates has been researched for some years. A frequently cited study of some years ago[1] produced research evidence that suggested the following:

1 Negative information is appropriately weighted but positive information is not weighted heavily enough.

2 Interviewers have a 'generalized ideal applicant' against which

interviewees are judged and which is, at least partially, unique to the interviewer.

3   By utilizing a job/person specification, the effect of irrelevant information is decreased.

4   Individual interviewers are not aware of the cues that they are responding to.

5   Visual cues, however, are more important than verbal cues.

6   Interviewers who perceive interviewees as being attitudinally and racially similar to themselves rate them as more competent and worthy of higher salaries, but were not more likely to recommend them for employment.

7   Similarity of sex between interviewer and interviewee has little effect on interviewer rating.

8   Training can remove the errors caused by the contrast between interviewee and others being interviewed on the same occasion.

9   Experienced interviewers are no more reliable than inexperienced interviewers in the data they produce.

10   The use of a structure in the interview helps interviewers remember factual data and improves reliability between interviewers.

Each of these stands up on its own as an interesting insight into what does or does not influence the interviewer, but as a view of the decision-making process it is a little fragmented. Unfortunately, as was mentioned in Chapter 10, much subsequent work in this area has turned out to be inconclusive and ambiguous.[2] But this does not mean it should be totally ignored. One of the results of the disappointment with these investigations has been that, more recently, researchers have taken a rather different approach to this area of decision-making.

The assumption is that the selection interview, like other interactions, provides a structured framework within which the interviewer attempts to understand the causes of the past actions and present behaviours of the applicant, and to assess future potential by linking them in a series of complex causal attributions. In other words, the interviewer is asking himself the question 'What appears to be the cause of these things happening to the candidate and are there implications here for future job performance?'. The suggestion is that there are four relevant causal attributions here.[3] They are ability and effort, which are seen as being within the person and thus internal, and luck and task difficulty, which are outside the person and thus external. Individuals tend to attribute their own success to internal factors and failure to external factors. Similar attributions will be made by individuals of others whom they like, but the reverse will be made of others who are disliked.

Thus, interviewers who like the interviewees will deem them to be personally responsible for their successes but not their failures, but with interviewees who are not liked the opposite will be the case.[4]

Further, it appears that attributions can be a function of what the interviewer expects of the candidate. Clearly, a main source of these expectancies might be the information on the application form, references, and/or the scores from tests taken prior to the interview. Or it may be that the interviewer has expectations which relate to the role of the interviewee, that is he expects interviewees to behave in a certain way.[5]

One experimental study has suggested that an interviewer with an unfavourable expectancy is likely to give the applicant less credit for past successes and hold the applicant more personally responsible for past failures. Also, the final decision to accept or reject applicants is closely related to these causal interpretations of past outcomes.[6] The importance for selection interviewing is that faulty expectancies can cause inaccurate decisions, because inferences have been drawn from the wrong data rather than wrong decisions made from the correct data.

If the view of the attribution theorists is to be accepted, it causes practical problems. How can the interviewer properly prepare for the task without being subject to idiosyncratic expectations? The solution is twofold. Firstly, interviewers should be trained to agree with the candidate the purpose and content of the interview. This involves drawing up a 'contract'. It was described as one of the interviewing 'rules' in Chapter 10. This removes some of the ambiguity of expectation between the interviewer and interviewee.

Secondly, the interviewer should be made aware of the long-term outcomes of his or her interviewing decisions. This may have the effect of modifying inaccurate expectancies, for example, he or she may learn that those with the very best university records are not necessarily going to become the most coveted employees.

Decision-making and testing

It is a frequent practice for test results to be fed into the interview as additional data to help the interviewer with his or her planning. However, some selection decisions are made on test results alone. These are where the test is being used as a screening device, allowing sufficiently high scorers to go on to be interviewed, or, less usually, where it follows the interview, which has assessed general suitability, to test for some specific ability. In these cases the accuracy of the test score becomes paramount.

What must be remembered is that the actual behaviour that a test measures is the ability to take that test. Any other behavioural implication, be it related to ability or personality, is by inference only. Therefore, for decisions of this kind to be made, that inference requires some powerful statistical backing, that is a high degree of predictive validity, suggested by a high correlation between test performance and job performance.

It has been suggested on a number of occasions in this book that the interpretation of selection test results is more difficult than it might appear, and often requires the skill of a suitably trained psychologist. To illustrate the point see Example 11.2.

Example 11.2

An organization wishes to employ an additional systems analyst. It has found that a standardized measure of verbal reasoning correlates r = 0.4 with an acceptable measure of job performance (this would be quite high by selection testing standards). Being overwhelmed with applicants, it decides to administer this test and interview to only the top 10 per cent of scorers; thus the decision is being taken not to select 90 per cent of the applicants, based on the test score. This raises two problems. Firstly, what is 'verbal reasoning'? It can be defined as the ability to solve problems using words and numbers, but does that really help? Why precisely should it relate in this way with the actual job of the systems analyst. Secondly, what does the correlation of r = 0.4 mean? What is it telling us? Or, more to the point, what is it hiding?

It is necessary here to introduce the concept of *common variance*. This is the extent to which two or more variables share a common explanation for being as they are. This can be expressed (for statistical reasons beyond the brief of this book) as a percentage by squaring ten times the correlation coefficient; thus a correlation of:

$$0.4 \times 10 = 4 \qquad 4^2 = 16 = 16\%$$

In this case, therefore, there is 16 per cent common variance between the verbal reasoning test and the measure of job performance for a systems analyst; or to express it the other way round, 84 per cent is not common, that is 84 per cent of what causes people to perform successfully as systems analysts is not being measured by the psychological test, yet it is being used as a major influence on decision-making.

A pitfall, therefore, of making selection decisions based on test results is failure to appreciate what the apparently simple statistic is really indicating. The effect of this is often to over-estimate the value of the prediction. (For a full discussion of this see Chapters 3 and 4.)

It is a common, and often necessary, practice amongst selectors who use tests, to identify cut-off scores which indicate the minimum level of test performance that is acceptable. (The part that test validity plays in determining where a cut-off point should be is discussed in Chapter 3.)

The existence of a cut-off score can cause, however, all applicants who score above it to be deemed as 'qualified', with final selection decisions being based on other factors. If a highly valid test is being used, such an approach will result in high scorers (the 'highly qualified') having no greater chance of selection than those scoring just above the cut-off point (the 'barely qualified'). This means the loss of potentially very able performers at the job.

To prevent this, the suggestion has been made that selection should be from the 'top down', that is the highest scorer is the first to be offered a job, the next highest the second, and so on until the vacancies are filled.[7] This will maximize the productivity of employees selected. The danger here is that it might unfairly discriminate against groups that exist within the applicant population, for example ethnic or sexual groups. But this can be overcome if these groups are identified and 'top-down' selection is conducted within each of them.

If a selector can say, with confidence, that the test he is using is highly valid and he is aware of any different levels of performance, on the test, between the groups that make up the applicant population, then 'top-down' selection not only makes sense, it is less unfairly discriminatory than other methods. If he is not confident, then it can prove to be an inaccurate and illegal way of making selection decisions based on test results.

Practical approaches to improving decision-making

Many individuals faced with the task of selecting people, especially for the first time, seek highly prescriptive aids to decision-making. Statements concerning universally desirable or undesirable aspects of any candidate are looked for, for example: Never select frequent job changers; Always hire those who can demonstrate flexibility, etc. In truth, these cannot be provided. There are no 'good' or 'bad' characteristics which are relevant to every job, and certainly not in isolation.

It is, however, possible to highlight some practical steps which can be taken to help decision-making to be more accurate.

1 Within the limits of administrative constraints, design the selection procedure to contain a small number of large, comprehensive stages (or hurdles) rather than a large number of small ones.

2 Check that the application form is adequate for the type of candidate who is likely to apply.

3   Train interviewers to make 'contracts' with interviewees to reduce the effect of inappropriate attributions.

4   Carefully identify, within the job and/or the organization being recruited for, the important behavioural aspects of successful performance. Then seek evidence of these behaviours in the present or past record of the candidate.

5   Consider precisely what aspect of a candidate is being measured by any standardized tests. This particularly applies to psychological tests. Do not make generalized assumptions from specific test results.

6   Use validated multiple methods, for example assessment centres, where feasible. These have the advantage of being designed to ease decision-making.

All of these steps are discussed, at some length, elsewhere in this book.

Structural aids to decision-making

As it is a major objective of selection methods to provide information about a candidate, it is important that this is interpreted, at least, with some degree of consistency. This can be aided by using a structured form.

The format used at the job analysis stage should provide this. For example, if the job analysis checklist (JAC) has been utilized (see Example 7.2), the data on each candidate should be re-evaluated against the fourteen headings, with special attention given to the performance of the main duties commanding the highest weightings. Candidates can be directly compared with each other to see those who have the most suitable personal attributes as required by the job as specified.

The benefit of returning to the job analysis at this stage cannot be over-emphasized. There is a tendency amongst some selectors to use the job/person specification only at the early stages of the selection procedure. Returning to it, physically, at the decision-making stage imposes a discipline. This can correct a tendency to re-specify the job in line with the attributes of the most 'liked' candidate. It is easy to lose sight of what is really wanted in the face of the vast amounts of information that selection methods can produce.

Some selection decisions, of course, cannot be made on the basis of a job analysis, because candidates are not being hired into specific jobs. The decision is between those candidates best suited to the organization and those not (an example is graduate recruitment). Selectors are seeking those with the most suitable qualities rather than those best able to perform a task.

In this case, the exercise which was used to elicit organizational criteria can form the basis of rating scales (see Example 7.1). Each candidate is assessed, by selectors, on these. An example of how part of such a set of scales might look is shown in Figure 10. In this example, candidates rated towards X more than Y will be those selected.

It is imperative that any rating scales (as with these examples) have at least one end of each scale expressed as a short statement of behaviour. Both ends should not be just abstract concepts. The meaning would be less clear and, as an aid to stable decision-making, it could become self-defeating. For example, it may be difficult for a number of selectors to decide, with consistency, the rating a candidate should get on a scale:

Flexibility _____ Rigidity

Each could have a very different view of what these actually looked like in job performance terms.

Decision-making by candidates

At a time when the belief is that jobs are scarce, it is easy to assume that the offer of a job will be followed by an acceptance. This assumption is dangerous.

The large multinational organizations which offer attractive career prospects for graduates are finding that as many as one out of three offers to new graduates is rejected. One of the reasons, as discussed earlier in this book, is that the employers are often competing for the same people. They are in a scarcer labour market than it appears. But candidates can reject offers because of the treatment they have received during selection.

Whatever the reason, candidates have a decision-making role that must be allowed for.

The normal practice is to attempt to forecast the offer acceptance/rejection rate by checking past trends, for example if 30 per cent of offers were rejected last year, then the assumption can be made that it will happen this year.

If there are no data to allow for this, or if it is a situation where one post is being filled, then it becomes the job of the interviewer to actively seek to gain information in order to make this judgement. The interviewer, as selector, must ask himself or herself not only 'Will this candidate be able to do the job successfully?' but 'Will this candidate accept an offer if one is made?'.

The common solution to the problem is to make offers to more people than need to be employed. It is a gamble and, as such, may not pay off. What do you do if all the offers are taken up?

Large organizations can often absorb the extra numbers, justifying it on the grounds that they will have a continuing demand for employees of this type. They are just hiring people a little ahead of when they need them.

X	X	Tendency to X	Unclear	Tendency to Y	Y	Y
'Considers the job to be more than nine to five working'						'Undedicated'
'Prepared to wait for promotion opportunities'						'Highly ambitious'
'Confident'						'Easily persuaded to alter decisions'
'Socially skilled'						'Has little influence on the behaviour of subordinates'
etc.			etc.			etc.

Figure 10 *Rating scale for assessing candidate performance against organizational criteria*

For the small employer, or where no assumptions about continuing demand can be made, the solution is less easy. One course of action is to withdraw some of the offers. Legally the employer has considerable scope to do this – even if they have been accepted. This, in itself, does not constitute a contract of employment and, as such, is not covered by this area of legislation.

Needless to say, to treat applicants in this way reflects badly on the employer and could damage future recruitment – even with regard to totally different jobs.

In practice, the small employer should adopt the following course of action:

1 Reject immediately, at the end of the selection process, only those definitely unsuitable.

2 Make offers to the successful candidates.

3 Hold over the remaining candidates on a reserve list. These should be informed that the final decision has not been made.

4 If any offers are rejected or ignored, then an offer can be made to someone at the top of the reserve list.

This procedure has to be carefully managed. Those made an offer must accept or reject it by a given date, and this must be adhered to. Those held over on the reserve list must be allocated to the 'offer' or 'reject' groups as quickly as possible.

Paying careful attention to this activity is better than being forced to either commence the whole selection cycle again or to make offers to those who have already been informed of their rejection. The first is costly, the second difficult to do without appearing foolish.

Other assessments in the decision-making process

Selection decisions are often subject to other specialist assessments. To pass a medical examination is a common requirement. Less often, candidates are subjected to security screening.

Failure at these stages can present problems for the selector if they occur after an offer has been made.

The Health and Safety at Work Act of 1974 has focused employers' attention on ensuring that employees are medically fit enough to perform their jobs. This includes not only the performance of heavy manual work, but also the ability to cope with stress. For this reason, the decision of a medical adviser carries a great deal of weight and is difficult to overrule.

To the candidate who is rejected after receiving an offer 'subject to medical' it is quite clear on what grounds the decision has been taken, but it is likely to be unclear, and extremely worrying why it should be. Such candidates really should have an individually drafted letter. This should explain in broad terms why their medical condition renders them unsuitable.

The problem can be avoided by medical references being taken up from their general practitioner, to supplement a medical questionnaire completed by the candidate himself or herself. This information can be acquired before an offer is made, and can replace the need for an employer-financed medical examination.

Similarly, security screening, where possible, should be carried out before offers are made.

Summary

Collecting accurate information about a candidate is one thing: deciding whether to offer a job on the basis of it is another.

Research on how interviewers make decisions has traditionally been fragmented and rather unhelpful. A current trend is to examine the preconceptions that interviewers have about the attributes of candidates. This has highlighted the possibility that inferences are made from the wrong data rather than the wrong decisions coming from the correct data.

Test results provide useful and accurate information, but it is easy to make wrong decisions by over-generalizing from what is essentially a narrow view of the candidate.

Universally applicable qualities which indicate 'good' or 'bad' candidates do not exist. But it is possible to take practical steps to make decision-making more effective.

The major aid to stable decision-making is a structured job analysis which should be re-consulted at this stage. Where this is not possible, rating scales, with behavioural statements, can be used.

Candidates reject offers, and this should be planned for. Similarly, an otherwise suitable applicant may be rejected on medical grounds. This can cause difficulties if an offer has already been made.

References

1 E. C. Webster, *Decision Making in the Employment Interview* (Montreal: Eagle 1964).
2 N. Schmidt, 'Social and situational determinants of interview decisions: Implications for the employment interview', *Personnel Psychology*, **29** (1976), p. 79–101.
 R. D. Arvey and J. E. Campion, 'The employment interview: a summary and review of recent literature', *Personnel Psychology*, **35** (1982), p. 281–322.
3 F. Heider, *The Psychology of Interpersonal Relations* (Holt Rinehart and Winston 1958).
 B. Weiner, *Achievement Motivation and Attribution Theory* (Morristown, NJ: General Learning Press 1974).
4 F. Medway and C. Lowe, 'The effect of stimulus person values on divergent self-other

attributions for success and failure', *Journal of Research in Personality*, **10** (1976), p. 266–78.

5 P. Herriot, 'Towards an attribution theory of the selection interview', *Journal of Occupational Psychology*, **52** (1981), p. 311–24.

6 D. H. Tucker and P. M. Rowe, 'Relations between expectancy, causal attributions and final hiring decisions in the employment interview', *Journal of Applied Psychology*, **64**, no. 1 (1979), p. 27–34.

7 F. L. Schmidt and J. E. Hunter, 'Employment testing – Old theories and new research findings', *American Psychologist*, **36**, no. 10 (1980), p. 1128–37.

12
Validating and evaluating the recruitment and selection procedure

The function of this last chapter is to step outside the system so as to take an overall view of the recruitment and selection procedure. This procedure, as a simple system, is shown in Figure 11.

Many people working in the field of selection would feel that this model logically depicts how things ought to be done. Indeed, this is the case. But its simplicity should not disguise the two very important issues which need to be considered. Firstly, validity, that is, does the procedure actually work?; and, secondly, evaluation, that is, has it all been worthwhile anyway?

Validating the recruitment and selection procedure

As the practice of recruitment has been defined, throughout this text, as the specific activity of acquiring a pool of applicants from which suitable employees can be selected, the validity of a recruitment method can be assessed by considering how successful it does this. This is discussed in Chapter 7. The degree to which any method produces candidates who can perform the job well is difficult to judge. The process of selection distorts any attempt to view the direct relationship between recruitment, as defined, and subsequent job performance. For this reason, the thrust of validation must be directed towards selection.

In selection validation there appears to be a paradox, namely a method should not be used unless there is evidence that it actually works. But how can this be known until it has been used? The answer is to follow the procedure of most technological developments, that is develop a prototype which is used, but not allowed to perform its assigned function within the system. We can take as an example the procedure for trying out a selection test. It should be included within the selection procedure so that candidates actually take it, but the results should not be used as part of the selection decision-making. Instead, these results are subsequently compared with job performance to see if this particular selection method has some predictive qualities. If it does, then it has been 'validated' for use in the future.

In practice, this creates a problem. A selector may have difficulty in

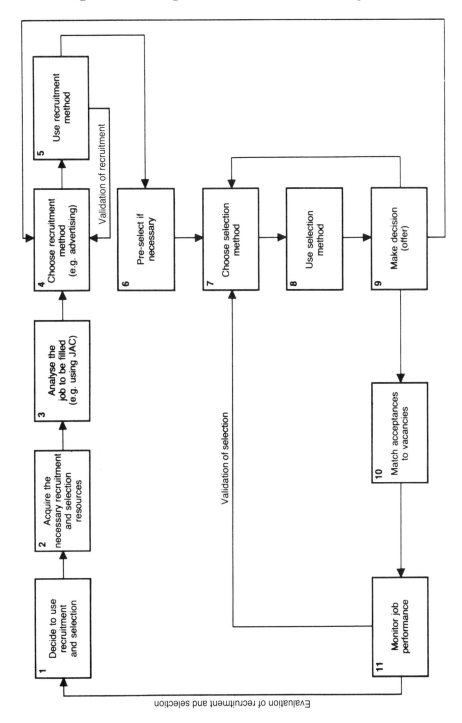

Figure 11   *A simple systematic recruitment and selection model*

convincing an organization that the methods which are being tried out in the selection of hirings will require some considerable period of subsequent job performance before it is possible to see whether these methods work and can be formally adopted. For trainee appointments such as apprentices or graduate hirings, this period can be as long as four or five years. For this reason, methods are frequently not checked for their *predictive* validity.

A compromise is to ascertain their *concurrent* validity. The test is administered to existing job incumbents, then their performance on it is compared to how they stand on a measure of job performance. The advantage of concurrent validation is that the comparison can be made immediately. For an explanation of different types of validation consider Example 12.1.

Example 12.1

An insurance company wishes to investigate the validity of a clerical aptitude test in the selection of 'clerical assistants'. Time is short. Thus, to administer the test to all new applicants and then wait some months to see if those who turn out to be the best clerical assistants are those who scored highly on the test, is administratively inconvenient. It is not feasible to measure *predictive* validity. Instead, it is decided to assess the job performance level of clerical assistants already employed. This group of employees is requested to take the clerical aptitude test. The scores on this are compared with the job performance 'scores'. If there is a tendency for the high test scorers to be the best job performers, and the low test scorers to be those who do their job less well, then it can be said that this clerical aptitude test has demonstrable *concurrent* validity.

Where possible, predictive validity should be ascertained rather than concurrent validity, as the whole reason for validation is to see if a selection method does predict.

In the case referred to in Example 12.1, and all the way through this book, wherever there has been mention of the importance of validating selection predictors, there has been reference to the uses of 'a measure of job performance'. The development of job performance criteria can present many difficulties. It requires some comment.

Job performance criteria
As was mentioned in Chapter 3, a job performance criterion must, just as a predictor must, be both a reliable and a valid measure. But against what

do you validate the criterion measure? To validate it against the predictor measure would, of course, be a nonsense. The quick and easy approach is to accept the criterion measure on one of the following grounds:

1 Face validity: 'It looks like a reasonable measure of job performance'.

2 Consensus of opinion: 'Everyone agrees that it is a good measure'.

3 Common sense: 'How can it not be a good measure of performance?'

But all of these, without further justification, are unacceptable – just as they would be if applied to a predictor measure such as a selection test. Alternatively, a different measure of job performance could be used to validate a criterion, but then why is it necessary to develop a second one?

The greater the non-repetitive character of the job, the greater the criterion problem. This is especially true for those jobs containing some managerial elements. Consider the case of the jobs of Section Heads in a large invoicing department in a commercial organization. Which Section Head is performing the best? The one whose staff process the greatest number of invoices? Or is it the one whose staff are guilty of the fewest errors? Maybe it is the Section Head whose staff have the best absentee record, or the lowest staff turnover rate. Naturally, it is likely to be a combination of some, or all, of these, but how should they each be weighted? One answer is that careful consideration should be given to the various aspects of job performance and simple subjective weightings applied. This may be helpful but still potentially fraught with error.

What is much more likely, however, is that not even this would be attempted. Rather, a single, simple rating by someone more senior in the organization would be used, thus providing another example of a measure of dubious validity. The concern here is that bosses have differing degrees of 'liking' for different subordinates, and differing levels of knowledge of their work performance.

One cynical counter to this criticism is that a subjective rating undertaken by a boss is, by definition, valid, because an organization will often only be able to reward performance if it is recognized by that immediate supervisor.

It is hard to understand why so many people endeavouring to develop a valid selection procedure should devote so much attention to the predictor and so little to the criterion. As one author has expressed it,[1] 'All too frequently, subjective classification, arbitrary grades or unreliable performance ratings are gratuitously accepted. One cannot expect to obtain acceptable validities with unreliable criteria.'

An approach which may provide some benefit to those attempting to validate selection methods is to recognize the extent of the criterion problem, and appreciate that the actual criteria that they are forced to use will never match the hypothetical ultimate criteria that they would like to have at their disposal.[2] The 'actual' criteria are only truly relevant to the extent that they coincide with the 'ultimate' criteria. Because of this lack of coincidence, the criterion measure actually being used will be deficient, since there are some important aspects of job performance not being assessed by it. Further, it is contaminated by aspects of the job which it does not want to reward positively.

For example, the performance of a salesman may be judged on his volume of sales. This criterion measure is used because it is accessible and quantifiable. It is deficient, however, in as much as it fails to assess the degree to which he promotes the good name of the company, and the contribution he makes to the harmonious running of the sales team. It is contaminated because it is measuring, positively, sales attained by aggressive, cavalier methods, regardless of damage to the company's name, and those achieved by using unfair tactics against his fellow salesmen.

A further constraint in acquiring reliable and valid criterion measures is that the search, for the sake of convenience, is all too often for a single measure. While it would be nice to find, it might be a fruitless search. As one often-quoted authority expressed it,[3] 'Much selection and validation research has gone astray because of an over-zealous worshipping of the criterion with an accompanying will-o'-the wisp searching for the best single measure of job success. The result has been an over-simplification of the complexities involved in test validation and the prediction of employee success.' This suggests, in our example of the invoice department Section Head, that the ability to manage staff so that they produce a high quantity of invoices is unrelated to the ability to minimize staff turnover; thus it would be unreasonable to compound these two elements as part of a measure of job performance. Instead, it might be more fruitful to validate separate selection methods against the manifestation of each ability.

Although the criterion problem can be considered the 'Achilles' heel' of scientific rigour in selection, this does not mean that it is negated, nor indeed, that it is totally unsolvable. In attempting a solution, the following are potentially useful sources of data:

1   Production records – providing both information on quantity and quality. It is a mistake to think these can only be usefully applied to production workers. They can be generated in most cases where work measurement is feasible, for example clerical workers, secretaries, telephonists, sales people, draughtsmen, maintenance personnel, etc.

2   Pay and promotion records – these can be useful since they represent decisions, usually taken after careful consideration of an individual's performance.

3   Personnel records – these will show absence, timekeeping, and labour turnover, which are often converted into cost criteria.

4 Formalized performance ratings – while straightforward subjective ratings by a boss are often used (and ratings by peers very occasionally), they may exist anyway as part of a systematic staff appraisal or 'management by objectives' scheme.

In addition, if the job being recruited for is that of a trainee, then additional criteria such as in-training academic performance, or the effectiveness of project work, can be included.

Each of these sources of criterion data has inherent reliability and validity problems, which are sufficiently self-evident not to need expansion here. But to dismiss them out of hand is tantamount to declaring the validation of recruitment and selection a non-starter.

Undertaking validation

Following on from the discussion in Chapter 3, the actual practices in carrying out a statistically based validation exercise are as follows: (NB As validation requires not only statistical knowledge but an understanding of the measurement of psychological variables, the services of a professional psychologist may be useful.)

Ensuring correct scaling It is essential that both the predictor and the criterion are represented as interval scales, that is, they are made up of units of equal size and are not simply rank orders.

Checking for correct distributions By 'correct' what is meant is 'normal'. The sample of hirings being used in the validation should have scores on both the predictor and the criterion which indicate that the average performance on both is around the middle of the scale, with the bulk of the sample being evenly distributed around that average, progressively tailing off. It should be extremely rare for individuals to be at the top or bottom of either scale. If, for example, it is shown to be the case that the hirings being used in this validation all scored maximum or near-maximum marks in a selection test, then the lack of 'normality' in the distribution will contaminate subsequent statistical analysis, for example it may make the correlation coefficient difficult to interpret.

Checking reliablity It is necessary that there be some evidence indicating the stability or reliablity of the measure being used. The score that an individual gets on either the predictor or the criterion must reflect their real performance, and not be a temporary quirk of the scale being used. Predictors such as standardized tests are easily coped with in this context, as reliablity evidence is often offered by the test authors in published form. The problem areas are, firstly, where subjective individual ratings are used as a predictor, or, secondly, where broad judgements, without guidelines, are made by someone such as a senior manager, and used as the criterion measure. This was mentioned earlier.

Using single predictors   Just about the simplest statistical model is one which takes a single predictor and assesses the degree to which it is associated with criterion performance – the degree of association being indicated by a high positive correlation coefficient (r). Thus, if there exists an acceptable measure of job performance, which can be applied to a group of employees who had previously taken a test at the time of selection, then that test can be validated to assess its powers of prediction. That is, as long as the conditions above have been met. There are various ways of computing a correlation coefficient of this kind, but the following formula is offered, because, although it might appear a little lengthy, it can be more easily followed than many others.

$$r = \frac{N\Sigma XY - (\Sigma X)(\Sigma Y)}{\sqrt{[N\Sigma X^2 - (\Sigma X)^2] [N\Sigma Y^2 - (\Sigma Y)^2]}}$$

Where: r is the coefficient of correlation
      N is the number of hirings featured in this validation study
      X is the actual predictor score of an individual
      Y is the actual criterion score of an individual
      Σ is the notation meaning 'sum of'

An observation which is often made on validity studies of this kind is the impossibility of building into the calculations data on candidates who are measured by the predictor but not hired. It is, however, statistically possible to adjust the correlation coefficient to compensate for the fact that the full range of candidates is lost through rejection at the selection stage.[4] It is important to note that this adjustment does not indicate how well rejected candidates might subsequently have performed.

Using dual predictors   The point was made in Chapter 3 that it is frequently the case that more than one predictor is used. It should be remembered that if selection decisions are made following an interview, which has been preceded by a carefully validated selection test, this does not constitute a carefully validated selection procedure if the same rigour has not been applied to the interview. Where there are two predictors in a selection procedure (for example, a test and an interview), then to validate this procedure as a whole requires that the following are ascertained:

1   The extent to which each predictor separately correlates with the criterion.

2   The extent to which the predictors correlate with each other.

If there is no correlation between predictors, then a multiple correlation coefficient (R) can be derived as follows:

$$R^2_{C.12} = r^2_{1C} + r^2_{2C}$$

Where: $R_{C.12}$ is the multiple correlation coefficient
r_{1C} is the correlation of the first predictor to the criterion
r_{2C} is the correlation of the second predictor to the criterion

Thus, the squared multiple validity is the sum of the squared individual validities.

Unfortunately, the relative simplicity of this is marred by the knowledge that predictors normally do relate to each other and this makes things more complex. If we take the example of a general intelligence test and an interview rating as the two predictors, then statistical evidence is hardly necessary to convince us that these two will produce scores that are related to each other. It would be especially true, due to attribution, if the interviewer was armed with the test scores before commencing the interview (see Chapter 11).

In order to overcome this problem, the multiple correlation coefficient must deal with the overlap between the two predictors, and this is achieved by the rather cumbersome extension of the formula above.

$$R^2_{Cc.12} = \frac{r^2_{1C} + r^2_{2C} - 2r_{12}r_{1C}r_{2C}}{1 - r^2_{12}}$$

Remember, this applies to only two predictors. If more than this number are involved, then the use of multiple correlation for validating the selection procedure will require the aid of a computer and the relevant statistical software.

Using multiple predictors   Where a whole range of selection methods are used, then it becomes important to know how good each is at predicting job performance, so as to know which of the devices should have the greatest influence on the selection decision. For example if scored application forms, references, a battery of tests and interviews are all being used, how valid is the information each provides.[5] Chapter 3 made reference to multiple regression, and this is the usual basis for this kind of multiple prediction. As mentioned in that chapter, this method makes certain assumptions about the nature of the relationship between predictors and criteria which can, by their very nature, be a source of some error. They are:

1   That the relationship between predictor and criterion is linear.

2   The central trade-off idea: that a low score on one of the selection methods can be compensated by a high score on another.

It is assumption '1' that is necessary for multiple regression to work. In fact, multiple regression is an extension of the one predictor approach that uses a single correlation coefficient. Two variables, for example a predictor and a criterion measure, are assumed to be linearly related and so the straight line which best fits the scatter of the cases when graphically represented (see Figures 1 to 4 in Chapter 3) is plotted. If there is, to any degree, a positive relationship between the predictor and the criterion, then the line would cut the Y (criterion) axis and start to climb at a fixed rate against the increasing values on the X (predictor) axis, reflecting that increased values of X represent increasing values of Y (for example, the better job performance scores are achieved by those with better selection test scores). A basic formula to describe that straight line is:

$$Y = a + bx$$

Where: Y is the predicted score on the criterion
a is a constant indicating the point at which the straight line crosses the Y axis
b is the slope of the line, or the change in Y observed for a corresponding change in x
x is the observed score on the predictor

If a further predictor is to be considered as well, for example an additional selection test, it is likely to have a different slope and produce a different predictor observation, thus another b shown as b_2 and another x shown as x_2. A third predictor would be b_3 and x_3 and so on. Therefore an n predictor model, where n is the final potential predictor of job success, can be shown by the following simple expansion:

$$Y = a + b_1x_1 + b_2x_2 + b_3x_3 \ldots \ldots \ldots b_nx_n$$

Multiple regression uses this expansion but modifies it by assuming that all the straight lines cut the Y axis at zero, therefore $a = 0$ and can be omitted. The multiple regression model thus takes the form:

$$Y = b_1x_1 + b_2x_2 + b_3x_3 \ldots \ldots \ldots b_nx_n$$

It can be seen that the computation rapidly becomes complex and soon requires computing facilities. As with multiple correlation, those wishing to undertake this type of validation exercise should seek out the relevant pre-packaged software.[6,7]

The above discussion is not intended to provide the necessary information to enable multiple prediction to be undertaken in this way, but to give an appreciation of what this kind of approach is actually trying to do. The resulting values, b_1 to b_n, indicate the weightings that should be applied to each of the predictors, X_1 to X_n, if they are going to be aggregated to provide a single measure of the predicted criterion score.

As an illustration, we can take a case concerning the selection of a computer programmer. Three predictors are used, each scored as a mark out of fifty.

Predictor one (X_1) is a selection interviewer's rating
Predictor two (X_2) is a verbal reasoning test score
Predictor three (X_3) is a computing aptitude test score

There is a linear relationship between these and a criterion measure (Y). This measure is the chief programmer's assessment of performance over a six-month period.

This relationship is expressed as the change in a job performance score observed for a corresponding change in test score (that is, the slope of the regression line) which is *b*.

If it is found, for example, that the expression is:

$$Y = (0.5)x_1 + (2.0)x_2 + (4.0)x_3$$

this means that for each candidate his or her predicted job performance (criterion) score is half of the interview rating score awarded, plus twice the verbal reasoning score, plus four times the computing aptitude score.

Taking four candidates, the picture of their scores might be as shown in Table 3.

Table 3

	Interview rating (X_1)	Verbal test score (X_2)	Computer aptitude testing (X_3)
Candidate A	30	20	15
Candidate B	24	40	20
Candidate C	10	25	30
Candidate D	40	20	18

By weighting and summing the scores, the predicted criterion scores emerge as shown in Table 4.

Table 4

	Weighted interview rating (b_1X_1)	Weighted verbal test score (b_2X_2)	Weighted computer aptitude test score (b_3X_3)	Predicted criterion score Y
A	(0.5) 30 +	(2) 20 +	(4) 15 =	115
B	(0.5) 24 +	(2) 40 +	(4) 20 =	172
C	(0.5) 10 +	(2) 25 +	(4) 30 =	175
D	(0.5) 40 +	(2) 20 +	(4) 18 =	132

From these four candidates it would appear that candidate C is the most likely to perform the best on the criterion being used. Candidate A is the most likely to perform least well. It should be noted that A performed better at interview than C, but, in this case, as it has been demonstrated that the interview is less effective as a predictor than the computing aptitude test, it is the superior performance on the latter by C that gives this candidate the advantage.

A rather different approach to using multiple predictors is through a 'profile matching' system. This is carried out in the following way.

1   A number of predictors are identified and accepted as important.

2   A group of 'successful' employees is measured on these predictors.

3   A typical profile for the successful worker is then produced.

4   The profiles of applicants are matched against this typical profile.

On the face of it, this may seem to be a sensible and simple way of going about things and, as a crude indicator, might be satisfactory. Unfortunately it does present a problem. How do you match profiles? One method is to add together the distances between a candidate's score and the typical profile score at each point on the profile, selecting the candidate with the smallest total distance. Another method is to correlate the candidate's score with the scores on the typical profile. The problem that this creates, however, is indicated in Figure 12.

The distance measured would favour candidate A, as the actual scores are closest to those of 'successful' employees. The correlation method would favour candidate B, for the shape of the profile is the closest to that of 'successful' employees. In practice, the answer is a compromise by inspection, that is the profile which looks to be most acceptably like the typical profile.

The procedures which have been outlined above are cumbersome and time-consuming, but the movement is towards providing easily accessible computer aid in the form of statistical packages usable with desk-top micros. Also, there are a number of consulting organizations which will supply a personnel department with a computer terminal and easy instructions on how to feed in the necessary data, which are transmitted to a mainframe computer with highly sophisticated statistical resources (sometimes not even in the same country). This will respond with very easily understood results.

Evaluating the recruitment and selection procedure

Figure 11 indicates that recruitment and selection can be conceived of as a series of discrete stages. This can suggest that one approach to enhancing the scientific rigour of the procedure is to validate each stage

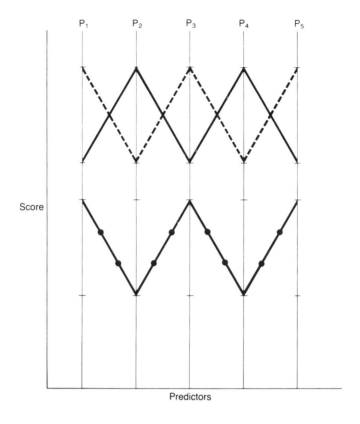

P_1 P_2 P_3 P_4 P_5

Score

Predictors

------- Typical profile of successful employee

——————— Candidate A

●————● Candidate B

Figure 12   *Profile matching using five predictors*

against the subsequent stage, instead of making a direct comparison with subsequent job performance. While this may be of practical value in tackling the problem of pre-selection, it is a dangerous practice as an overall strategy. Each stage, other than the first one, becomes itself a criterion measure, which by the very nature of the procedure is of unknown validity. Thus, there can be a serious compounding of error, resulting in almost nonsense by the final stages. What is much more useful is the *evaluation* of each stage in the context of the overall evaluation of the total procedure. In other words, the final question that must be asked of the procedure is 'Has it all been worthwhile?' and this question can be asked of each stage in relation to the next.

For example, the ease with which recruitment and selection resources can be acquired is one criterion which can be used to evaluate the initial decision to use recruitment and selection. Similarly, problems in drafting advertisements in part reflect on the way the job being recruited for has been defined. Further, the pre-selection issue is related to the efficiency of the recruitment method, and so on.

If the whole process is being undertaken by one person, then that individual must at each stage ask the question 'What could I have done at the previous stage in order to minimize the problems I am now faced with at this stage?'. It is, of course, likely that, through the inherent frustration in trying to do a good recruitment and selection job, this question has not been answered, or even posed.

In the situation where recruitment and selection is not a one-person operation, individual recruiters and selectors, be they personnel specialists or managers, often have to make the most of other people's decisions and actions. In such a case, the evaluation procedure dictates:

1   The problems encountered at any stage must be fed back to those operating the previous stages.
2   These individuals should acknowledge the problems and offer solutions which can include, but hopefully not as a matter of course, pointers to a fault in even earlier stages.

Consider the example of the organization which wishes to hire very capable graduates as trainee corporate planners, but finds, at the end of the recruitment and selection process, that the number of candidates accepting offers of employment is insufficient to meet the number of vacancies. In this case, the previous stage, that is making the selection decision, is undertaken by the corporate planning manager, after he has interviewed shortlisted candidates. The acceptance rate becomes, in part, an evaluation of this manager's contribution to the recruitment and selection process. On having the information about the low acceptance rate fed back to him, the manager undertakes to re-focus his interviewing. He will investigate each candidate's interest in offers received from other organizations and improve the way in which he highlights the attractive elements of his own organization. Part of the problem can be attributed as being further down the line. Pre-selection and recruitment practices could be modified to provide some candidates who are not so heavily sought after by other organizations. An important element of the above example involves the giving of feedback to interviewers. This is an aspect of evaluation which requires a special mention. Interviewers need to be informed of how valid their own decisions have been. This practice, which on the face of it is common sense, is, surprisingly, frequently ignored. Indeed, as has been mentioned several times in this text, the common practice of selectors, especially interviewers, not having to pay the price of bad decisions is a major cause of validation being considered unnecessary.

Interviewers should seek to become well aware of the subsequent performance of those whom they recommended for hire. This information must start to be fed back at the earliest time that it becomes discernible after the candidate has commenced employment.

In practical terms, the records of a new hiring should indicate the name of the interviewer, or interviewers, who made the selection decision. Where possible, these decisions should be monitored by using subsequent performance appraisal reports on the hirings.

This kind of stage-by-stage evaluation, which can be represented by taking Figure 11 and reversing the direction of the arrows, provides a useful internal check on the recruitment and selection process, but each stage does need to be considered against the ultimate job performance of selected candidates; for example, in Chapter 8 it was pointed out that a recruitment method can be evaluated in terms of the number of applicants it provides, but, in the end, it needs to be tested in terms of the quality of those eventually hired. Evaluating each stage against job performance can sometimes indicate gross misdirection of recruitment and selection effort, where costly and lengthy procedures in the end produce job incumbents who perform no better than if they had been acquired through a process of near abandonment.

Ultimately, the governing factor is likely to be cost, in as much as it represents 'value for money'. There are many hidden, or hypothetical, costs in making bad selection decisions which, by their very nature, are difficult to assess. (These were discussed in some detail in Chapter 1.) The extent to which any recruitment and selection procedure will reduce these is difficult to forecast. It is at the evaluation stage that this issue must be faced head-on. The question to be answered is 'Does the improved level of job performance warrant the amount of money invested in the procedure?' Because of the problem of satisfactorily measuring job performance, which can hide both benefits and costs in the short term, it is difficult to produce a quantified answer.

What cost evaluation can do is to indicate those parts of the procedure that are not giving value in cost/benefit terms.

Consider the example of the organization which wishes to improve the standard of management trainee that it employs. An existing selection procedure which involves the use of a single interview is replaced by an expensively designed assessment centre. It is found that there is no discernible improvement in the standard of trainee selected.

On investigation, it is discovered that the salary offered is so uncompetitive that selection is being undertaken from an unsatisfactory pool of applicants. The salary level cannot be sufficiently increased to resolve the problem, so the use of this selection method, on grounds of cost, is discontinued.

The first chapter of this book pointed out that recruitment and selection was one of several possible solutions to organizational problems. Evaluation is meant to determine whether it has achieved this. We return once more to the example mentioned at the beginning of Chapter 1 which was concerned with the high turnover of typists. If the solution that has been opted for is to pay special attention to the recruitment and selection of these employees, and, as a result, the problem has receded, then this would constitute a positive evaluation of the recruitment and selection procedure (as long as it does not create more problems that it solves). But if the high turnover continues, then the evaluation must indicate that it is not worthwhile, and that one of the other identified strategies may, with hindsight, be better.

Troubleshooting recruitment and selection problems

This final section is offered in recognition of the fact that even the most carefully prepared of procedures can go wrong. What is needed is an indication of where solutions to problems can, in the first instance, be sought. Example 12.2 should be considered as a 'guide to fault-finding'. The list of problems is, of course, not exhaustive and the solutions are simply suggested as the most likely. The chapters where these solutions are more fully discussed are indicated.

Example 12.2   *A guide to fault-finding*

Problem	Strategy for initial solution	Chapters to refer to
Not knowing the actual job the hiring will do	Focus on functional/ organizational criteria	7
No time to prepare proper job specification	Question the need to recruit and select	7 and 1
Difficulty in identifying the real key aspects of the job that recruiters and selectors should pay attention to	Use Job Analysis Checklist (JAC) with the Main Duties Weighting (MDW)	7
Concise advertisement is difficult to write	Use JAC and MDW	7
Advertisement produces a poor quality response	Reconsider where it has been placed	8
Advertisement produces too many applicants who withdraw during the selection process	Do not disguise negative aspects of the job in the copy	7 and 8

Advertisement proves very expensive in relation to the response it produces	Use publication that does not reach such a wide readership	8
Advertisement produces too large a response	Rewrite copy to include more detail	7 and 8
Too many applicants have responded	Set up pre-selection procedure	2 and 9
Pre-selection procedure is difficult to design	Seek valid predictors of job being offered from application form data	9
Only inexperienced interviewers are available	Introduce interviewer training	6
Key people are not available or willing to carry out interviews	Question the original decision to use recruitment and selection	1
Internal resources are not sufficient to undertake a temporary recruitment and selection drive	Use an outside agency	6
It is essential that specific, identifiable abilities must be assessed as accurately as possible	Use standardized validated tests	3, 4 and 10
Personality must be measured	Use a reliable and standardized personality questionnaire, interpreted by a suitably trained person with the results fed into the interview	3, 4 and 10
To be selected, general suitability is paramount	Use competent interviewers with training as necessary	3, 6 and 10
Knowing which predictive aspects of a candidate are the most useful to investigate during an interview	Those which indicate present or past behaviour that are relevant to the behaviours necessary to do the job	7 and 11
Selectors have to make some sense of psychological concepts	Outline what they mean, dispel common misconceptions and indicate problems of measurement	4

Problem	Strategy for initial solution	Chapters to refer to
What to do with information from references	Accept it only if the reference format is highly structured or the source is known to be valid	10
A candidate scores highly on tests but disappoints in the interview or *vice versa*	Re-consult JAC and MDW	7
Which selection method should be used when time and money are no real constraint?	Use multi-method group selection (assessment centre)	10
Which should be used if free to use board, sequential or single interviews?	Choose sequential interviews	10
For political reasons a board interview must be used	Do not allow membership to exceed four and carefully consider the role and influence of each member	10
The selection decision is, in the end, based on interview performance	Train interviewers in judgemental skills	3 and 6
A trained interviewer keeps making the same mistakes with his or her decisions	Ensure that information on these mistakes is fed back to the interviewer	12
Not enough job offers are accepted	Check content of recruitment phase and check interviewer's style and method	6 and 10
Knowing how many offers to make when the likely acceptance rate is unknown	Do not reject the near-misses until acceptances of offers have been received	11
Failed candidates strongly challenge the selection decision	Ensure methods are ethical and legal	5
Hired candidates have the ability but lack interest in the work	Probe the candidates' inclinations during the interview	4 and 10

Hired candidates are enthusiastic but lack ability	Do not allow a competent interview performance to necessarily override test results	10
New employees quit after a short period of time	Make sure that the negative aspects of the job are known to candidates during the recruitment and selection process	7, 8 and 10
Selection methods prove to be disappointing	Improved validation work has to be undertaken	3 and 12
Carrying out the recruitment and selection programme has not solved the organization's problem	Check validity of procedure. If reasonable, seek alternative solution	1 and 12

Summary

The validation of recruitment and selection is answering the question 'Does it work?' Evaluation is answering another 'Has it all been worthwhile?'

The major problem of validation concerns the criterion of job performance which is to be used to assess the predictive qualities of selection methods. The measures which are actually used are somewhat less suitable than are ultimately needed.

Validation methods are usually statistically based. They rest heavily on the principle of correlation. In practice, as most selection procedures involve more than one predictor, techniques such as multiple regression or 'profiling' are necessary.

If recruitment and selection is seen as a series of stages, it is possible to evaluate each of these in terms of the way that they affect the next stage. In the overall evaluation it is the consideration of cost effectiveness that is important.

References

1 P. Drenth, 'Principles of Selection', in *Psychology at Work*, P. B. Warr, (ed.) (Penguin 1978).
2 M. L. Blum and J. C. Naylor, *Industrial Psychology* (Harper & Row 1968).
3 M. D. Dunnette, 'A note on the criteria', *Journal of Applied Psychology*, **47** (1963), p. 251–4.

4 J. P. Guilford and B. Fruchter, *Fundamental Statistics in Psychology and Education*, 6th ed. (McGraw-Hill 1978).

5 A. Anastasi, *Psychological Testing*, 5th ed. (Macmillan 1982).

6 N. H. Nie, C. H. Hull, J. G. Jenkins, K. Steinbrenner and D. H. Brent, *Statistical Packages for the Social Sciences*, 2nd ed. (McGraw-Hill 1975).

7 C. H. Hull and N. H. Nie, *Statistical Packages for the Social Sciences – Update 7.9* (McGraw-Hill 1981).

Index